IN A PERSIAN MIRROR

IN A PERSIAN MIRROR

*Images of the
West and Westerners
in Iranian Fiction*

By M. R. Ghanoonparvar

University of Texas Press, Austin

First edition, 1993

Requests for permission to reproduce material from this work should be sent to Permissions, University of Texas Press, Box 7819, Austin, TX 78713-7819.

⊗ The paper used in this publication meets the minimum requirements of American National Standard for Information Sciences—Permanence of Paper for Printed Library Materials, ANSI Z39.48-1984.

For reasons of economy and speed this volume has been printed from camera-ready copy furnished by the author, who assumes full responsibility for its contents.

Library of Congress Cataloging-in-Publication Data

Ghanoonparvar, M. R. (Mohammad R.)
    In a Persian mirror : images of the West and Westerners in Iranian fiction / by M.R. Ghanoonparvar. — 1st ed.
        p.   cm.
    Includes bibliographical references and index.
    ISBN 0-292-72760-7 (alk. paper). — ISBN 0-292-72761-5 (pbk. : alk. paper)
    1. Civilization, Western in literature.   2. Persian fiction—19th century—History and criticism.   3. Persian fiction—20th century—History and criticism.   I. Title.
    PK6424.C58G48   1993
    891'.5509321821—dc20   92-39689

To the memory of my father

CONTENTS

PREFACE AND ACKNOWLEDGMENTS

The seeds of the present study began to germinate in the late 1970s and early 1980s, while I was working on a book entitled *Prophets of Doom: Literature as a Socio-Political Phenomenon in Modern Iran* (1984), during which time relations between Iran and the West, particularly the United States, had reached a critical point. The Islamic Revolution of 1979 had already taken an anti-Western turn. On television screens around the world, nightly scenes of the revolution in Iran, with crowds of Iranians shouting anti-American slogans, blared the message of apparent disdain, even hatred. American flags were set ablaze and effigies of Uncle Sam were burned. Anti-American sentiments were also verbalized and promoted by the officials of the revolution; indeed the central figure in the uprising, Ayatollah Ruhollah Khomeini, proclaimed the United States the "Great Satan." More significantly, with the occupation of the United States Embassy in Tehran, termed the "Spy Nest," by a group of revolutionaries calling themselves the "Students Following the Line of the Imam [Khomeini]," relations between the two countries, in fact, relations between Iran and the West in general, were brought to the brink of crisis.

My own research on and reading of modernist Persian literature at the time, for the purpose of completing the aforementioned monograph, drew me constantly to justifying in my own mind the relevance of writing about Persian literature in English for an American audience. After all, would not most Americans, indeed my potential readers, be expected to respond negatively to all things Iranian, including Persian literature, given the current anti-American actions and sentiments of Iranians? At the same time, however, as a student of literature, I was intrigued by the manifestation of the anti-Western sentiments in Iran, so often presented in symbolic form. Attacks against such symbols as the American flag and Uncle Sam and depictions of the United States in the form of the awesome image of the Great Satan compelled me to seek out such symbolism and try to determine the roots of the ongoing reactions to the West in Persian fiction, which has dealt by and large, directly or indirectly, with socio-political issues and inevitably with the political and cultural interrelationship and interactions with the West.

More than a decade has passed since the upheavals began in Iran, and many writers, including former politicians, political activists, and scholars, have made strides to shed light on the origins and causes of the discord between Iran and the West. In terms of understanding the roots of this conflict, some research has been done and much more is needed by historians and social scientists. In recent years, an increasing number of scholars have engaged in such studies from the perspective of a variety of disciplines. A few examples are: R. K. Ramazani's *The United States and Iran: The Patterns of Influence* (1982); Nasrin Rahimieh's *Oriental Responses to the West: Comparative Essays in Select Writers from the Muslim World* (1990); Mehrzad Boroujerdi's *Iranian Intellectuals and the West: A Study in Orientalism in Reverse* (1993); and Mohamad Tavakoli-Targhi's *Women of the West Imagined: Occidentalism and Exotic Europeans* (1993). These and other studies provide a background and an explanation of the basis of the attitudes of Iranians toward the West and contribute to an understanding of the perceptions of Iranians in regard to the West. The present study, however, focuses on one particular aspect of this issue. Through an examination of the works of a number of Iranian writers, I explore the perceptions of the West and Westerners of these writers as they have dealt with the subject in their works. More specifically, I attempt to probe the questions: When a Western character appears in a story, how is he or she portrayed? And how are Western societies and Western civilization presented in these works? In other words, what are the images of the West and Westerners that appear in the mirror of Persian fiction?

The terms West, Western, and Westerner as they appear in this study may need some clarification. The West that is the subject of this book is not always marked by specific geographical boundaries. It is sometimes represented by a single country and at times is shaped, even though artificially, in a particular work as the story dictates. This flexible notion of the West also extends to that of its inhabitants who are presented as characters in these stories. Nevertheless, despite the vagueness of the usage of these terms, a general definition of the West and Westerners as they appear in the material examined in this study can be garnered. England, France, and Germany as well as smaller countries such as Belgium and Switzerland are included in these writers' notion of the West. There is, however, at different periods of history ambiguity with regard to Spain and even Italy. On the other hand, Russia, both before and after the Bolshevik Revolution, generally conjures up the West in the mind of Iranians. On the other side of the Atlantic, the United States and Canada are certainly regarded as a part of the West, while Latin America is for the most part excluded from this definition.

The publication of Edward Said's polemical and theoretical work, *Orientalism*, in the late 1970s gave rise to much critical thinking about the relationship between the West and the "Orient," which, Said argues, meant the Middle East and India to Orientalists. It may be tempting for readers to think of a study such as the present work as a book on "Occidentalism," or an Eastern counterpart to "Orientalism." Even though readers may find in the attitudes and perceptions of Iranian writers the other side of the "Orientalism" coin, so to speak, it should be kept in mind that such attitudes and perceptions were neither institutionalized nor formalized, which was the case, according to Said, with regard to Orientalism.

I have refrained in the present study from deriving any particular theories about the images of the West and Westerners in the collective or individual psyche of Iranians. That should be left to the reader. My conclusions in the final chapter should be taken simply as a summation of the stories discussed in this book, although I beg the reader's indulgence for a few introspective words about the nature of literature and literary scholarship in Iran.

By and large, the works that are analyzed in this study are by major Iranian writers. The focus has inevitably led me to examine hundreds of short stories and novels containing Western characters or direct characterizations and depictions of the West. Obviously, I have had to select a relatively small number of these works, those which I believe are representative of the literature dealing with this subject, for inclusion in this study. For readers not familiar with Persian, an attempt has been made to identify those works which are available in English translation. More detailed bibliographic information on these works has been included in the endnotes and bibliography.

The transliteration of all Persian words and names is based on Persian pronunciation and follows a modified version of Naser Sharifi's system in *Cataloging Persian Works*, the exceptions being: (1) diacritical marks are avoided, such as those which distinguish between different consonants pronounced alike in Persian and represented by different letters or over vowels, and (2) the apostrophe (') is used to represent both the letter *eyn* and the sign *hamzeh*, but is omitted in the initial position. All translations from the Persian are my own, unless otherwise stated. I have, however, followed the preferred spellings with regard to the names of certain writers who have also published in English, in materials quoted from English language sources, and for Iranian names with standardized spellings in English.

In the course of the years since I began this project, I have been most fortunate to have been able to discuss my research on this subject with colleagues and students from many institutions on a variety of occasions. I have presented papers on numerous aspects of this topic at the University of Virginia (1984), the University of California at Berkeley (1986), the Annual Meeting of the Middle East Studies Association of North America in Baltimore (1987), the University of Michigan (1988), the University of Arizona (1989), and the Annual Meeting of the Texas Association of Middle East Scholars in Austin (1989).

The initial grant for this project came from the University of Virginia in the summer of 1983. A major portion of the research and writing of the book was done during the 1988–1989 academic year which I spent as a fellow in the Rockefeller Residency Program in Middle Eastern Languages and Literatures at the University of Michigan in Ann Arbor. The program, which was called "A Window to the Issues and Values of Contemporary Middle Eastern Societies of Value to Others Who Are Not Familiar with Relevant Middle Eastern Languages or Literatures," especially suited my work at the time. I am particularly thankful to the director of the Center for Middle East Studies at the University of Michigan, Professor Ernest McCarus, the Center staff, and the many friends, colleagues, and students who made it possible for me to enjoy a most productive and rewarding year in Ann Arbor. I am likewise grateful to the Rockefeller Foundation for its financial support during that year. In the summer of 1991, I received a Research Award from the University of Texas, which enabled me to complete my research and prepare the final draft of the book.

Friends and colleagues throughout these years have extended their support and have most graciously shared their ideas. Professor Hafez Farmayan of the University of Texas at Austin has been continually generous with his knowledge of Iranian history, particularly nineteenth-century travel diaries, of which I have made extensive use in this volume. At various stages, I have benefited from the comments of numerous other colleagues, Leonardo Alishan, H. Q. Azadanloo, Michael Beard, Mehrzad Boroujerdi, Hamid Dabashi, Veena Deo, Faridoun Farrokh, John Green, Quay Grigg, Michael Hillmann, M. A. Jazayery, Mehdi Nourian, Roger Savory, Mohamad Tavakoli-Targhi and Gernot Windfuhr, among others, some of whom have read parts or all of this work. Their advice and insight have helped improve it, although I must personally accept the responsibility for any and all shortcomings evident in this study. A note of thanks goes to numerous other friends, both in and outside Iran, including Abazar Sepehri, the head of the Middle East Collection at the Perry Casteneda Library at the University of Texas, and Ali Dehbashi, the chief editor of *Kelk* journal, who have helped me locate the materials needed for this book. To all of them I am most grateful.

I would like to express my appreciation to the very professional staff of the University of Texas Press, particularly Frankie W. Westbrook, and also Theresa Wingfield, Nancy Warrington, and Carolyn Cates Wylie. I am also indebted to the meticulous copy editing skills of Elli Puffe.

Finally, my deepest gratitude goes to my wife, Diane, for her indispensable wordprocessing skills and for her undiminished patience with me during the many years that have gone into the completion of the project.

1

INTRODUCTION

The extreme anti-Western actions and reactions of Iranians over the past decade have been the cause of not only dismay but astonishment to a great majority of people, experts and laymen alike. Although the mass media and the public at large have often responded to, even dismissed, this phenomenon as strange and irrational, to a growing number of dispassionate social scientists and other scholars, this seemingly puzzling phenomenon is becoming more comprehensible in terms of the intercultural relations between Iran and the Western world. One key to understanding such actions and reactions lies in the way Iranians have viewed the West and Westerners both traditionally and, more importantly, in modern times. An important source in any examination of these views is imaginative literature, which, as an artistic representation of life, touches on the intangible roots of human attitudes, actions, and reactions in ways peculiar to the creative arts in general. Accordingly, imaginative literature, more specifically prose fiction, can be studied and analyzed not only in aesthetic terms or as a social phenomenon, but also as a window, as it were, into aspects of human life often overlooked by other fields of human knowledge. In the same vein, literary works can serve as an important aid in understanding cross-cultural impressions and can provide valuable insight into the roots of intercultural discord.

The present study is an examination of the images of the West and Westerners as revealed in the works of Iranian writers of fiction, in particular selected representative travel diaries, novels, and short stories. The approach is descriptive rather than polemical. Two basic questions are inherent in this inquiry: How have Iranians, or more accurately, certain Iranian writers, viewed the West and Westerners? And, what are the justifications for the particular positive and negative reactions of Iranians to the West? While the answers to the first question are addressed explicitly in this study, the answers to the second are dealt with indirectly and implicitly, for the most part.

Although references are made to other genres and periods, the study concentrates primarily on twentieth-century Persian fiction. The focus on this specific genre and period is dictated by the very nature and concerns of modern Persian fiction, which claims contemporary society and social and human issues as its main theme. While classical Persian literature, as characterized by many proponents of modernism, consisted for the most part of panegyric and didactic verse or was written on such themes as mystical love, modernist Persian literature departs fundamentally from this tradition, shifting its focus to the more mundane, to social issues and the lives and concerns of the common people of the society. With this departure, poetry, which had been the nearly exclusive genre of the literary writing of previous centuries, gave way to prose fiction as a more appropriate means for literary artists to write about and communicate to larger segments of the population. At the same time, the increasing exposure of Iranians to the outside world, particularly the West, and the dilemmas which they faced in attempting to absorb the forces of modernity without totally abandoning their traditional values and way of life have been among the major concerns of virtually every contemporary Iranian writer of fiction.[1] In their attempt to respond to the forces of modernity and external influences, Iranian writers have portrayed Western characters in their work, and the West and Western values and those who espouse them have become recurrent features of this literary genre.

The images of the West and Westerners in the Iranian consciousness have not been formed suddenly or in the course of only a few years. Certain attitudes appeared and evolved through previous centuries which continue to have at least some degree of influence over the picture Iranians have shaped in their minds of the West and its inhabitants today.

Two Persian terms, *farang* and *farangi*, have been in use in Iran for many centuries. Etymologically "France" and "French," respectively, in the past *farang* and *farangi*, often rather vague in usage, have commonly referred to the people and lands of Christendom, generally including Byzantium. In recent times, particularly since the late eighteenth and early nineteenth centuries, these terms have gradually acquired less ambiguous meanings and now refer to the West and Westerners in general, more specifically to the lands and peoples of Europe and North America.

Direct mention of the term *farang* in classical Persian literature is infrequent.[2] The renowned thirteenth-century poet Sa'di uses the term *farang* on only a few occasions, in which case it generally connotes a hostile image of the Other, as in the following didactic anecdote from the *Bustan* [translated into English as *Morals Pointed and Tales Adorned: The "Bustan" of Sa'di*], in which he warns his readers against the evils of slander. The dervish in the story, upon hearing a man besmirching another, has already decided before questioning the slanderer how to condemn him, by equating him with the enemy, the Franks, telling him that his words are like the weapons of the enemy when used against the Moslems:

> Some knowers of the Way, firm-footed,
> Sat in solitude a while together;
> Then one of their number embarked on calumny,
> Opening the door to mention of a wretched fellow.
> To him one said: "Colleague of addled dye!
> Have you campaigned against the Franks at any time?"
> And he: "From out my own four walls,
> I've never in my life set foot!"
> At this spoke that *darvish* of candid breath:
> "Never I saw one of such reverted fortune:
> The infidel sits safe from his assault,
> The Muslim can't escape the cruelty of his tongue!"[3]

The question asked of the man accused of issuing his malicious statement appears rather irrelevant in the context of the anecdote. Sa'di uses it to lead up to his concluding lines, an aphorism of sorts in which the infidels are said to be safe from the man's attack while Moslems are victims of his wicked tongue. The image that is reflected of the *farangi* is not only that of an enemy against whom Moslems should fight, but synonymous with infidel, an equation that the reader must take for granted.

In his *Golestan* [translated into English as *Gulistan or Flower Garden*], Sa'di uses the term in an anecdote on his travels to the Holy Land, where he is taken prisoner by the *farangi*s and forced to dig ditches. An acquaintance, who happens to see him, takes pity on him and pays for his release. He ultimately marries his rescuer's daughter, whom Sa'di describes as a "termagant and vixen" and who makes his life miserable. In response to the reproach of the wife, declaring that her father had saved her husband from captivity by the *farangi*s, Sa'di likens the situation to that of being delivered from the clutches of wolves and given over to a woman worse than a wolf.[4]

In both anecdotes, the image that emerges of the *farangi* is a hostile one, of people who are at war with the Moslems. Although in neither case are they the main target of his criticism, the *farangi*s are used by Sa'di to invoke a negative image with which to compare a character he intends to portray as wicked.

In the famous episode, "Sheykh San'an," of Faridoddin Attar's *Manteq ot-Teyr* [translated into English as *The Conference of the Birds*], no mention is made of the two terms in question; however, the story reveals the perceptions of a twelfth-thirteenth-century Iranian poet about Christians and Christendom.

The story of Sheykh San'an is a parable that involves a Sufi elder who has led a life of piety and asceticism for some fifty years. For several nights he dreams that he is in Rome or Byzantium and is worshipping an idol, an act repugnant to any devout, monotheistic Moslem. Compelled to unearth the significance of this gnawing dream, accompanied by his followers, he journeys to Rome where he beholds a beautiful Christian girl and falls passionately and uncontrollably in love with her. Ignoring the counsel of his followers, the sheikh submits to the demands of the beloved, who will accept him on the condition that he abandon his faith in Islam, worship the icon, burn the Koran, and partake of wine. He submits, but the beloved still refuses to accept him, for he is poor, and she further demands that he tend her swine herd for a year. In the meantime, the sheikh's followers, stunned by his unthinkable behavior and led by a pious devotee of the sheikh, pray to God for the release of their elder from the enchantment of the Christian girl. Their prayers are answered when the pious devotee dreams that the Prophet has opened the sheikh's eyes to the truth once again and has restored his faith to him. The story ends with another dream, this time for the Christian girl, who also comes to understand the nature of true love, repents her cruelty to the sheikh, converts to Islam, and dies.[5]

We should not, of course, detract from a conventional reading of the parable in the context of Persian mystic poetry, in which the example of the sheikh's love for the Christian girl shows the path of mystic love to Sufi disciples. But there is also in the poem an implied (perhaps subconscious) negative image of the Christian Other, a premise upon which the parable is constructed.

The dichotomy established in Sa'di's anecdote and Attar's story between Moslem and Christian, the Islamic world and the non-Islamic Christian world, is the dichotomy between the Self and the Other, both, in this case, characterized by religious beliefs. The Islamic world of the sheikh and his followers in Attar's story is one of spirituality and belief in the Islamic God and the path of truth, whereas the Christian world, by way of contrast, is one of idol-worshipping, wine drinking, and materialism. This dichotomy is a reflection of that which existed in the Moslem mind in the past, the dichotomy of *dar al-Eslam* [the abode of Islam] and *dar al-harb* [the abode of war, or the enemy].[6] While the sheikh and his followers belong to the former, the Christian girl belongs to the latter.

The image of the Christian Other in the Persian mystic mirror of Attar's poem, is, of course, distorted, as it does not—and is not intended to—reflect the spiritual side of the non-Moslem Other. Even so, such images of the Christian Other generally associated with the vaguely defined notion of the *farangi* [or Western] Other not only reflected Iranian views of *farang* and *farangi* but also helped perpetuate such notions about this Other throughout the cultural history of Iran.[7] The vagueness of the image of the West in the past was obviously due to the limited contacts between Iranians and the West. The lack of knowledge about the West on the part of Iranians and their eagerness to learn about it would become apparent to Western travelers and diplomats who visited the country in the early nineteenth century. One such visitor was James Morier, a British diplomat, who reflected the contemporary Iranian views about the West in his 1824 picaresque novel, *The Adventures of Hajji Baba of Ispahan.*[8]

Morier's novel is in fact a vehicle through which the author records his impressions of the Iranian society of his time by placing his protagonist in various situations and circumstances. At one point, Hajji Baba becomes a confidant of the king's ambassador, who is charged by the monarch to learn what he can about *farangestan*, or the West, in general. The task in turn is conferred on Hajji Baba by the ambassador, who furnishes him with an abstract of the king's decree. The protagonist-narrator recounts that:

The ambassador was, in the first place, enjoined to discover, in truth, what was the extent of that country called Frangistan; and if the Shah known in Persia by the name of the *Shahi Frank*, or king of the Franks, actually existed, and which was his capital.

In the second place, he was ordered to discover how many *Ils*, or tribes, of Franks there were; whether they were divided into *Shehernisheens* and *Sahranisheens*, inhabitants of towns and dwellers of the desert, as in Persia; who were their khans, and how governed.

Thirdly, to inquire what was the extent of France; whether it was a tribe of the Franks or a separate kingdom, and who was the infidel Boonapoort [Bonaparte], calling himself emperor of that country.

In the fourth place, his attention was to be turned particularly to what regarded the Ingliz [English], who had long been known in Persia, by means of their broadcloth, watches, and pen-knives. He was to inquire what description of infidels they were, whether they lived in an island all the year round, without possessing any *kishlak* (warm region) to migrate to in the summer, and whether most of them did not inhabit ships and eat fish; and if they did live there, how it happened that they had obtained possession of India; and he was to clear up that question so long agitated in Persia, how England and London were connected, whether England was part of London, or London part of England.

In the fifth place, he was commanded to bring positive intelligence of who and what the *Coompani* [East India Company] was of whom so much was said—how connected with England—whether an old woman, as sometimes reported, or whether it consisted of many old women; and whether the account, which was credited, of its never dying, like the lama of Thibet, were not a fable. He was also enjoined to clear up certain unintelligible accounts of the manner in which England was governed.

In the sixth place, some positive information concerning *Yengi duniah*, or the New World, was much wanted, and he was to devote part of his attention to that subject.

> Lastly, he was ordered to write a general history
> of the Franks, and to inquire what would be the
> easiest method of making them renounce pork and
> wine, and converting them to the true and holy faith,
> that is, to the religion of Islam.[9]

Those familiar with Iranian history and Iran's relations with the West in 1824, when *The Adventures of Hajji Baba of Ispahan* was first published, would interpret Morier's depiction of the Iranian king's ignorance in regards to the West as humorously exaggerated. The character of Hajji Baba as a confidence man and his adventures, which would have appeared very odd to Morier's British readers, contribute to the creation of the context required for such humor at the expense of an "Oriental" king. At the same time, Morier's presentation of the king's perceptions and misperceptions about Europe reflect various basic truths rooted in earlier images existing in the minds of Moslems regarding the inhabitants of "the abode of the enemy," or Christian Europe. The imprint of such images of the West and Westerners from the past lingered in the minds of early Iranian travelers to Europe and America, in the eighteenth and particularly the nineteenth and twentieth centuries, and in greater numbers than ever before, they recorded their impressions of those places, their inhabitants, their beliefs, and ways of life in the popular literary and historical genre of the time, the *safarnameh*, or "travel diary." Chapter 2, "Understanding the Unknown," examines a number of these travel diaries by Iranian travelers to the West, not merely as historical documents but as imaginative records of how the West and Westerners were seen directly through the eyes of these Iranian visitors. The genre of the travel diary has been a focus of scrutiny by social scientists, particularly historians, for the purpose of reconstructing the Iranian history of the past century. In recent years, especially since the Islamic Revolution, a greater number of these accounts have been edited and published. For literary scholars, they have usually served as texts studied for the prose style of a particular period. However, one aspect of these works that has been ignored is their place in Persian literature as a precursor to modern fiction, not merely in terms of prose style but, perhaps more importantly, in terms of their contribution to the art of story telling. In other words, even though these *safarnameh*s purport to be objective accounts of the writers' observations, they are in many respects fictional reconstructions of the West in which the writers, wittingly or unwittingly, present a picture colored by their own preconceived cultural notions of the West and Westerners.

With the increasing exposure of Iranians to the West and the political, social, and cultural influences of the West on Iran which seemed inevitable to many educated Iranians came some degree of understanding of the West.[10] The prevailing image of the West and Western societies began to change from the somewhat monolithic, vague, and exotic Other generally regarded with hostility to that of an Other, albeit still alien, whose advancements in social, technological, and even political arenas educated Iranians in particular found appealing. Among this group were proponents of total emulation of the West and a complete transformation of the society to the Western model. Having seen firsthand or learned about the advancements made in the West, these Iranians believed that the same formulas that had worked in Europe, for instance, in building a prosperous society could also be utilized and implemented in their own country. So taken with the West were some of them that not only did they desire the restructuring of Iran socially and politically to resemble Western societies, but they even proposed Western-style reforms for the very appearance of the society, the shape of the cities, and the manner of the people's dress. A natural reaction to this position came from those who saw the inherent danger of such blind emulation which would, they argued, result in the loss of political independence and cultural identity. The battle between traditionalists and modernists occurred in various forms and in various arenas in the society and spread to virtually all social institutions, even to the realm of literature itself. The reflections of such ideas and the intellectual conflicts evident in the Iranian prose fiction of the twentieth century are examined in Chapter 3, "The West in Contrast," and Chapter 4, "The Xenophobic Impact." One-dimensional images of the West do appear in the works of these authors who were motivated by xenophobic impulses, but such images should not suggest that the picture presented by these literary artists is simplistic or monolithic. While the perspectives of writers espousing extremist political views, particularly in the second half of this century, are generally negative—characterizing, even stereotyping, Westerners as imperialists and the West as the breeding ground of imperialism—careful scrutiny of these works shows that such views are nonetheless in the minority. This is also true of writers on the other end of the spectrum, that is, those who idealize the West and find the solution to all their country's problems in emulating and identifying with it. The predominant view, however, seems to be one of ambivalence toward the West and Westerners on the part of writers who present both positive and negative aspects as they see them. But even such ambivalence is not uniform, which is to say that the attitudes of literary artists differ from region to region and period to period and are inevitably linked to the writer's own background and experience. The reaction of writers from regions such as the Persian Gulf area, who have had a longer history of direct contact with foreigners and for whom Westerners have been less of an oddity, for instance, differs markedly from that of writers in other parts of the country, where such contacts have been rare or even nonexistent. In the same vein, the attitudes of literary artists change with events such as the fall of the popularly supported nationalist government of Dr. Mohammad Mosaddeq in 1953, which is generally blamed on the West, particularly the United States.[11] A sampling of stories displaying such an ambivalent attitude is examined in Chapter 5, "Split Images."

Another aspect of the literary characterization of the West and Westerners in Persian prose fiction can be illustrated in what Iranians of various classes and backgrounds have understood the West to be and in their efforts to emulate or reject what they have interpreted as Western values and ways. Reza Shah Pahlavi's efforts to "modernize" Iran are clear examples of his understanding (or misunderstanding) of the West and Western progress.[12] Perhaps the most controversial example of such efforts was his 1936 banning of the traditional veil for women.[13] In his opinion, shared by many Westernized Iranians of the time, the advancement of women in the West was directly related to their not being veiled. Although many Iranian intellectuals of his and the following generations, literary artists included, ridiculed and even condemned Reza Shah Pahlavi's drastic measures to modernize (or as he apparently saw it, Westernize) Iran, their own understanding of the West and Westerners as well as the reasons behind the advancement of the West did not differ significantly in many respects either in degree or kind from those of Reza Shah Pahlavi.

A swing of the pendulum from the fascination with the West of Reza Shah Pahlavi and his son, Mohammad Reza Shah Pahlavi, and their Westernization programs, undoubtedly a reaction to the direction in which the Pahlavis were leading the

Iranian society, came with the onslaught of the 1978–1979 Islamic Revolution in Iran, which brought with it fundamental changes. This revolution has been viewed as an anti-Western phenomenon, given the rampant revolutionary slogans and demonstrations as well as the hostile actions, propaganda, and generally negative attitude toward the West of the newly established government. Images such as the "Great Satan" in reference to the United States by Ayatollah Khomeini suggest that once again a negative monolithic picture has formed in or been imposed on the Iranian psyche.   As have other members of the society, writers have been affected by the politicized climate of the Iranian Revolution, which in turn has undoubtedly left its imprint on their work. The question of how susceptible recent fiction has been to such anti-Western sentiments is explored in Chapter 6, "Post-Revolutionary Reflections," through an analysis of novels and stories written in Iran since the Revolution.

Literary artists in every society are at times the unwitting victims of the propaganda of the regime in power. Once writers accept or reject the notions that a government tries to inculcate into the people, their work can be regarded as a reaction to such propaganda. Politicians and ideologues alike are unquestionably fond of black and white pictures, of good and evil portrayals. The creative artists themselves, not to mention the audience, the public at large, are not immune to such propaganda and often fall victim to it, accepting such transparent portrayals of good and evil and recreating them in their work.

To characterize the understanding of Iranian writers and their portrayal of the West and Westerners as totally naive and uninformed would, however, be unfair, not to mention naive and uninformed in turn. Western readers will find in the works of some writers portraits of themselves that are hardly recognizable. But the same readers will find many other Iranian authors who display in their works a fundamental knowledge of and familiarity with European and American ways of life and values and who are fully capable of creating revealing fictional situations in which Westerners and Iranians are juxtaposed, confronted, and compared. Ultimately, such comparisons can prove enlightening to students of the humanities in terms of providing a glimpse of the West and its inhabitants, values, and ways from the outside, as it were, a view which, though not consistently positive, nor even totally accurate, heightens our knowledge and awareness of both the observer and the observed.

2 UNDERSTANDING THE UNKNOWN

In the eighteenth and particularly the nineteenth centuries, the terms *farang* [taken from the word Frank; Europe or the West in general], its equivalent *farangestan* [literally the land of the Franks], and *farangi* [Western or Westerner] continued to be used as they had been earlier with reference to the lands and people in what could loosely be termed Christendom, in one sense, the areas and people that populated the domain of Western civilization. That is to say, the boundaries of *farang*, or the West, were not quite clearly defined in the minds of most Iranians. While, on the one hand, for the educated and the travelers to the West—who were relatively few but increasing in number—to identify a specific area as *farang* or a particular person or group of people as *farangi* would have been relatively easy, for the uninformed Iranian, on the other hand, *farang* was a wondrous, imaginary place found in popular traditional tales, a land of exotic objects and peculiar people with even queerer customs, not unlike the "Orient" has been to Westerners.[1] As one historian puts it, "It is the land of *A Thousand and One Nights*."[2] For the educated Iranian, the magic of *farang* derived from its progress and technological advancement. However, both groups viewed the West with a sense of wonder—the uninformed Iranian, as a story land, a fairy-tale world, and the better-informed observer as a futuristic, perhaps even ideal, model worthy of emulation.

Although the perceptions of the average Iranian about the West at the time are not readily accessible to us, because of the popularity of the genre of the *safarnameh*, or travel diary, from the eighteenth through the nineteenth and into the early twentieth centuries, we do have records of how relatively informed and knowledgeable Iranians perceived the West and Westerners. The *safarnameh* was by no means a new genre in

Iran. Famous Iranian men of letters such as Naser Khosrow had written their travel accounts in previous centuries.[3] Nevertheless, this genre gained such popularity during the reign of the Qajar Dynasty [1779–1925] in Iran that it dominated the prose literature of the time. During this period, numerous Iranian travelers to the West wrote about their experiences in *safarnameh*s, a number of which were required of officials making such trips on diplomatic, economic, trade, and technology exploration missions. Others were written by private individuals who traveled for a variety of reasons, including education, trade, curiosity, and a sense of adventure.[4]

Many of these travelers approached the West without specific information or knowledge about the lands and the peoples they were about to encounter. In a sense, many of them embarked on their journeys as if they were indeed visits to the mysterious *farang*, a sort of Aladdin-and-the-Magic-Lamp land. For this reason, these travel accounts show a consciousness on the part of virtually every traveler of the "otherness" of the people they encountered and the differences between Iran and the lands of *farangestan*. It should be kept in mind, however, that what these Iranian travelers perceived was filtered through a glass, as it were, tinted with certain preconceived notions inherited from the past and colored with their own personal and cultural beliefs and biases. Even so, the audience of such works would most likely accept these tinted images as accurate reflections of the West. To the critical reader, on the other hand, these images of the West are often more subjective than objective, closer to the fruit of the writers' envisioning of the West than the reality of what they actually witnessed. In other words, the West that is revealed in the *safarnameh* is but a reflection of the West, a mirror of a particular kind, the Persian cultural mirror of these Iranian travelers.

A cursory glance at these travel diaries shows that the impressions left by the West and Westerners on these writers are both positive and negative. The Self and the Other are at times explicitly and often implicitly compared and contrasted. Certain aspects of the Western Other Iranian visitors admire and describe with a sense of envy, yet at the same time other attributes of the Western societies, peoples, beliefs, and customs they find appalling. The Otherness of the West is particularly evident in the negative attributes of the West against which the Iranian travelers generally warn their compatriot readers.

One of the earliest travel diaries chronicling a trip to Europe is *Masir-e Talebi* or *The Safarnameh of Mirza Abu Taleb Khan*.[5] Mirza Abu Taleb embarks on a journey to England in the late eighteenth century, arriving in London in January of 1800. Born and reared in India, Mirza Abu Taleb, the son of Iranian parents, had been acquainted with a number of Englishmen and had worked for the East India Company in his youth. Provoked by English officials, Abu Taleb became involved in a quarrel with a rajah, whom he subsequently killed. Consequently, he felt compelled to flee the country for London, where he soon gained a footing in English "society," becoming known as the "Persian Prince."

Before he arrives in England, Mirza Abu Taleb's journey takes him through South Africa to Ireland, where he records his first impressions of Europe and Europeans. He gives detailed descriptions of the food, climate, buildings, city squares, theaters, city parks, churches, parliament, restaurants, horse races, and other aspects of life in Dublin and other cities that he finds interesting and feels would be novel for his readers. He compares the Irish people with the English and comments that, unlike the English, most of them are Roman Catholic. He adds that:

> [The Irish are] free of the immoderation of the
> "English" and the excessive piety and fanaticism of
> the "Scots" in following Christian religious laws; they
> are moderate. They are distinguished from the
> English and the Scots for their courage, bravery,
> spending, hospitality, kindness to strangers,
> friendliness, and kindheartedness. Although they lack
> the astute, firm wisdom of the English, they are
> superior to them in intelligence and quickness of
> wit.[6]

In support of these observations, the author then proceeds to describe his landlady and her children, who are ever willing to help and provide him with whatever he needs, even though he cannot speak English and has to resort to sign language. He further observes that "because of their carefree nature, spending a great deal, and devoting time to friends, the Irish have few wealthy people among them."[7] Unlike the English and the Scots, he observes, the Irish do not worry about poverty when they are not in need, "hence, they make little advancement in sciences and gaining social status." He also comments on the excessive drinking of the Irish, and that he had heard from the English that they get drunk at the dinner table and kill each other. "But," he reflects, "during my stay, I saw no impolite or inhumane action by them."[8]   In regard to the English, upon leaving Ireland, he is warned by his Irish friends that he will have difficulty in England, because the English will not be able to understand and help him.   After his journey to Europe, when he records his memoirs and impressions of England, he concurs with these remarks: "Although I had been in England for more than a year and learned English a hundred times better, they still could not understand me."[9]   These comments notwithstanding, his relatively lengthy stay in England is a fruitful one.

Soon after his arrival in London, Mirza Abu Taleb is given an audience with the king and queen of England, which in turn opens channels to the homes of the English nobility, about whose manners and customs he writes in detail.   It must be kept in mind that his observations about English society and his perceptions of how that society is structured and how it functions derive virtually exclusively from the perspective of the upper classes.[10]

Nevertheless, Mirza Abu Taleb is a keen observer and quite capable of pinpointing those aspects of the English society that distinguish it from the Eastern societies with which he is familiar.   He realizes, for instance, that in England the rule of law provides freedom for the people and protects them from tyrannical rule.   About English laws of freedom he writes: "The English have no fear of their rulers and superiors with regard to their [reputation or property], let alone for their lives, provided they have not committed a violation."[11]   What impresses him as indicative of freedom is that "in contrast to India, the nobility can walk in the streets, go to shops to ask the price of goods, and purchase them," or "they can go to the houses of prostitutes to spend the night and take their wives or mistresses by the hand and go in their company for a stroll in the parks." Furthermore, "they publicly express the faults of their kings and ministers verbally, in illustrations and in books."   Mirza Abu Taleb confesses: "In my whole life, I had never strolled in the streets or gone to a shop, let alone to the houses of women.   In finding such freedom, I felt so relieved, as if a very heavy burden had been lifted from my shoulders, as if I had been in shackles and was now freed."[12]   As he understands it, English freedom means that one "can do anything that would not harm anyone else or break a law, not that anyone can do whatever he pleases."[13]   The English are, according to Mirza Abu Taleb, quite rigid in upholding their religious and civil laws, and those who break them are seriously rejected by the society.   This extends even to social mores, as his example indicates: "If a person commits a slight infraction, such as eating at a low-class restaurant, they [his compatriots] shall never associate with him, let alone if he commits a serious violation."[14] In terms of the equality of the nobility and the common people, the author observes that such equality exists essentially in terms of dress, but there is less of a relationship between the two classes than exists in India.[15]   On the other hand, the commoners seem to have the upper hand in quarrels with prominent people. He tells a story of the crown prince who was brushed up against during his walk by an "impolite" commoner and had struck the man with his walking stick. The prince was then obliged to pay a fine to the court and compensation to the plaintiff.

One aspect of English society that would inevitably leave a lasting impression on such a visitor from the East as Mirza Abu Taleb concerns the role and function of women in that society. His observations and comments about the English attitude toward women at times appears contradictory, indicating a degree of vacillation in himself. He implicitly approves, for instance, of the relative "freedom" that English society affords women, even with regard to their being unveiled, especially in contrast to his own Moslem society, in which women were confined to the home, and public interaction between men and women was restricted.   In England he witnesses the visible involvement of women in various aspects of the society and praises the English for assigning certain jobs, such as shopkeeping, to women, but also for devising rules that "harness women to prevent them from engaging in immoral acts, despite the fact that they mingle with men and wear no veils."[16] Among these rules he mentions the custom of men outside family members being forbidden to visit women except at dinners and parties with many other people present, the prohibition against women visiting the homes of unmarried men, and their not being allowed to go out after dinner, "particularly to sleep in other than the husband's bed, even in their parents' home."[17]   He then compares the English attitude toward women with that of Moslems:

It becomes clear that despite their granting them

apparent freedom and engaging them in utmost
flattery, the English ... control their women wisely.
The Moslems, on the other hand, despite the custom
of veiling, which is a sort of control that induces
mischief and corruption, out of ignorance, offer them
opportunities for corruption by granting them control
over money and female servants and children and
allowing them to go to the homes of their parents
and relatives, even female friends, where they spend
weeks on end, day and night.[18]

Mirza Abu Taleb concludes his observations about the
English and English society by summing up their "virtues" and
"vices." Among their virtues he praises their sense of self
esteem, particularly among the upper classes; their respect for
and courteous attitude toward one another; their respect for the
law and adherence to the limitations placed on the rights of the
individual; the inclination of their thinkers toward that which
benefits the public at large and their abhorrence of that which
is detrimental to the society; their penchant for new clothing,
furniture, and other necessities, the result of which benefits the
craftsmen and encourages new inventions; their hospitality; and,
finally, their taste in terms of the appearance of buildings,
clothing, jewelry, and household furnishings, especially with
regard to colors and decorations, in terms of which, "with the
exception of some Iranians," they are superior to the rest of the
world.

On the other hand, he is critical of the English for their lack
of belief in religion and the Day of Judgment and their
inclination toward philosophy, which, he feels, has ill effects,
particularly on the lower classes. Furthermore, he observes, their
excessive pride results in a lack of farsightedness. For instance,
he says, as the result of high taxes there are riots which they
only try to put down by force, rather than thinking about the
long-term consequences. Among the vices of the English which
Mirza Abu Taleb disapproves are their love of worldly riches,
their fondness for comfort, their quickness to take offense when
their faults are pointed out to them, their proclivity for spending
an inordinate amount of time on sleep and personal appearances,
their excessive craving for luxuries, their lavish pleasure in food,
and their tendency to be opportunistic and exhibit false modesty
for personal gain. He also observes that the customs of girls
eloping with their lovers, premarital sexual relations, and lack of

control over lust have resulted in the proliferation of prostitutes. Because of their extreme pride, according to this traveler, the English consider their own customs, habits, and religion to be flawless and those of others erroneous. Moreover, he criticizes the English for their failure to appreciate the knowledge and languages of others, such that "as soon as they learn a few words [of a foreign language], they consider themselves expert linguists ... and engage in writing and publishing such utter nonsense."[19]

After spending about two and a half years in London, Mirza Abu Taleb sets out on his journey back to India. He spends two months in France which, in contrast to his stay in England, he does not enjoy. He describes the condition of the French villages and the life of the French peasantry as very harsh and quite horrible. Interestingly, he detests French food, declaring, for example, that they cook the meat over a hot fire for so long that it dries up and loses all its flavor. He comments: "During my two months in France, I did not enjoy more than five or six meals." He describes the coffee houses and restaurants as extremely filthy, with many beggars who surround the patrons and even "follow you into the restaurant." What is worse is the "large dogs in the restaurants, the number of which exceeds that of the beggars."[20]

Except for the appearance of the buildings in Paris, Mirza Abu Taleb finds very little to his liking in France. He describes buildings of seven or eight stories crowded with fifty to sixty people of higher and lower classes living in them. In contrast to England, everything appears to him to be filthy; streets are not properly lit; and prices are much higher than in London. Although he finds the French people courteous, easygoing, and cheerful, he criticizes them for their disorganization and failure to learn from experience to improve the condition of their daily lives.

Mirza Abu Taleb's travel diary was written after his return to India. Because of his association with the English in India prior to his departure for Europe as well as his relatively lengthy stay in England, and also given the animosity of the British toward the French at the time, the conclusion might be drawn that his impressions of France and French society were influenced to a great extent by the attitudes of his English hosts. But at the same time, despite his evident admiration for England and the English people, Mirza Abu Taleb has a keen eye and critically observes and comments on those aspects of the English society, customs, and beliefs of which he disapproves. The importance of *The Safarnameh of Mirza Abu Taleb Khan* is that it is one of the earliest firsthand accounts of the West written by an Iranian, a book which was widely read by educated Iranian travelers.[21] Nevertheless, the fact should be kept in mind that even though Mirza Abu Taleb was an Iranian and wrote his work in Persian, his frame of reference was to a great extent the Indian society of the time. Worthy of note, however, is the fact that the observations recorded in later *safarnameh*s written by Iranians with the Iran of their time as their frame of reference do not differ significantly in many respects from those of Mirza Abu Taleb.

One of the earliest of such *safarnameh*s was written by Mirza Saleh Shirazi, who traveled to Europe only a decade after Mirza Abu Taleb.[22] Mirza Saleh was one of a second group of students dispatched to England by Abbas Mirza, the Iranian crown prince, to study the new sciences, including engineering, medicine, chemistry, and military sciences. Mirza Saleh travels to England via Russia, where he spends some time writing about Russian society, particularly the schools and religious practices, and in some detail about Russian history. His memoirs of England, where he spends several years, on the other hand, deal mostly with his personal anguish in trying to cope with English officials under whose care Mirza Saleh and the other four Iranian students are placed. Caught in the web of English and Iranian government bureaucracy and, according to the author, the self-interest of their official British patron, who expects financial gain from this opportunity, these students are essentially left to their own devices for nearly three years. This account differs dramatically from that of Mirza Abu Taleb, whose encounters were mostly with the affluent classes and who was treated, as the name given him by the London newspapers suggests, as a "Persian Prince." The image of the English officials that emerges from the diary of Mirza Saleh is, therefore, rather negative and in some ways foreshadows the suspicious attitude of many Iranians of the following century, as is pointed out in the ensuing chapters of this study.

Nonetheless, Mirza Saleh is an impartial enough observer not to generalize his feelings about particular English officials to all English people. During a visit of a few weeks to the English countryside, where he is the guest of an English family, he finds an opportunity to praise the English for their kindness, generosity, good manners, hospitality, customs, education, and charity.   He also makes visits to various industrial and commercial centers and describes in some detail the wonders of Western progress, including paper factories, the shipping industry, textile factories, and mines.   He comments on the English system of government and devotes many pages to English history, its wars and even the discovery of America. Most intriguing, perhaps, are his perceptions of the English social system, based on his own personal impressions and experiences.   He often relates such impressions in the form of a simple, unpretentious anecdote through which his Iranian readers would have found an image of a Western society that was in sharp contrast to the social and political conditions of Iran in the nineteenth century.   One such anecdote involves the British prince regent, its thematic thrust being individual rights and freedom.   The prince regent orders a street to be built and named after him; however:

> A poor craftsman has a shop located in the middle of
> that alley. For six months, they have made every
> effort to convince him to give up his shop, but he
> refuses. Even if, for instance, the whole army were
> to surround him, he cannot be forced to leave his
> shop. What is interesting is that the prince himself is
> unable to harm him physically or financially. This is
> a country with such security and freedom that it is
> called the land of freedom. While there is freedom,
> there is a kind of government order that is adhered
> to by everyone, from king to beggar, and anyone who
> deviates from the laws is punished.[23]

Mirza Saleh is impressed most by the social services in England, among which he describes in detail schools, orphanages, insane asylums, the postal service, city parks, museums, libraries, theaters, restaurants, hotels, and transportation. Unlike his predecessor, Mirza Abu Taleb, Mirza Saleh possesses a sense of mission. In providing such intimate detail of Western progress, his conscious purpose is to inform his compatriots, at least those in the government who are more likely to read his travel report. One could surmise that Mirza Saleh's painstakingly recorded descriptions of the English government, including such details as the qualifications of those elected to the House of Commons, how decisions are made and implemented after the king and the parliament come to an agreement, and the judicial system in that country, were also intended as lessons to his prospective readers. Perhaps as the result of Mirza Saleh's sense of mission, throughout his travel diaries, he appears quite adamant that he not waste time in England but continue to learn. After a stay in England of more than three years and nine months, upon his departure he still feels that his studies remain incomplete, even though he has managed, among other things, to learn enough about the printing industry to take home a small printing press and later publish the first newspaper in Iran.[24]

Seemingly uninvolved, even unconcerned, about the political dealings taking place between Iran and Western governments, particularly England, Mirza Saleh portrays England as being more advanced in terms of societal and technological progress; yet, in comparing the culture and customs of his own country with those of England, he refrains from moral judgments, merely stating that they are different and that he prefers his own. It is perhaps because of this preference that he often insists on wearing his Iranian clothes and, unlike Mirza Abu Taleb, avoids getting involved in English social life. He has a singular purpose in most of his associations with the English, which is the acquisition of the Western knowledge he believes will prove useful in his own country. In contrast to Mirza Abu Taleb, again, he avoids giving stereotypical descriptions of the English people. When, for instance, he is displeased with the way he is treated by the English officials, his criticism is directed towards particular individuals, and his praise for others is based on specific examples and the character of certain people with whom he comes in contact. In other words, in Mirza Saleh's *safarnameh*, there seems to be an attempt at impartiality, even though obviously his cultural biases, even if subconsciously, play a role in his portrayal of English society.

In contrast to the travel diary of Mirza Saleh Shirazi is *Heyratnameh* [*The Book of Wonders*] by Abolhasan Khan Ilchi, the Iranian ambassador to the English court who traveled to London a few months before Mirza Saleh left England.[25]

Despite the fact that Abolhasan Khan considers himself well-traveled and quite familiar with various cultures and societies, he is more out of place in and unfamiliar with English society, even after his nine-month visit to London, than is Mirza Saleh, who is much younger and lacks his experience. And although Abolhasan Khan's is essentially a diplomatic mission, unlike Mirza Saleh he seems to be oblivious to anything pertaining to

Western progress. He devotes countless pages to describing beautiful women and his flirtations with them, or to the luxurious lifestyle of the English nobility. Even during a visit to the House of Commons, his main comment concerns the simplicity of the decor, "two candles lit in two candlesticks on a table in front of the scribes," with which he is not impressed.[26]

A major objective of the author of The Book of Wonders, as its title suggests, is to present aspects of the West that would entertain the reader, mostly by reporting on strange and astonishing customs or objects. For this reason, whatever new invention or machine the ambassador describes is mentioned merely as an object of amazement, the description being devoid of the intense curiosity that characterizes the commentary of many other writers of travel diaries before or after him. This aspect of The Book of Wonders reinforces the conventional notion of the dichotomy between the Self and the Other. Nonetheless, on certain occasions Abolhasan Khan makes an apparent attempt to see the similarities between his own culture and that of the English. Upon describing English religious marriage ceremonies and the laws governing marriage in that society, for example, he comments: "What became apparent to me is that the religious faith of other Westerners is quite different from that of the English people. Rather [the differences] are like those of the Shi'ite and Sunni faiths. In other words, the rest of the Europeans are Sunnis, and they [the English] are the Shi'ites [followers] of the prophecy of Jesus."[27]

Although Abolhasan Khan is often conscious of being out of place, even an oddity, in English society, on several occasions in comparing the customs of his own culture with those of his hosts, he prefers those of the latter and openly wishes that his compatriots would learn from the English. On one occasion he writes: "In my opinion ... if the people of Iran were to have the opportunity to emulate the ways of the English people, they would prosper in all the affairs of their lives."[28] This is a sentiment echoed later on by a number of prominent Iranians advocating total emulation of the West. Most nineteenth-century Iranian travelers to the West, however, are more cautious in their attitude toward the West and the unqualified imitation of it.

Abolhasan Khan's limited vision of the West, and the fact that he is oblivious to Western social and political progress and scientific and technological advancement, may have been the result of his own egotistic and essentially hedonistic character, and does not represent the attitudes of most Iranian travelers to the West.[29] While it is true that most Iranian writers of travel diaries are fascinated by the appearance, dress, and social involvement of Western women and the freedom that they perceive in the relations between men and women compared to their own society, at the same time, they are interested as much, if not more, in other aspects of the West. This can be seen, for instance, in *Makhzan ol-Vaqaye'* [*The Treasury of Events*], the travel diary of Farrokh Khan Aminoddowleh, who visited Europe in the mid-nineteenth century.[30]

Like Abolhasan Khan, Aminoddowleh was also on a diplomatic mission, indeed a more important and urgent one, but unlike his predecessor he provides us with a comparatively comprehensive portrayal of the West and Westerners.[31] This may be due in part to the fact that the diary of Aminoddowleh's visit to Europe was written by a professional scribe who accompanied him solely for this purpose.[32]

As a statesman, Aminoddowleh is interested in garnering information on military matters, such as the discipline of soldiers, their uniforms, and their weapons; in the parliamentary government system; the irrigation methods and agriculture; paved roads; the railroads and the heating of rail cars with hot water pipes; the public toilets found on the streets and in parks; the educational system, prisons, insane asylums, and other public services; as well as the customs regarding hospitality, the relations between men and women, mannerisms, and familial relationships. In France, on his journey from Marseilles to Paris, he sees prosperous villages and cities, all of which seem connected to one another, leaving the impression of one large city:

> There is little land in this country, but many rich
> people. You cannot find a small patch of land that is
> not owned by someone or is uncultivated. All
> villages, orchards, and homes are built in a uniform
> and organized manner, because in this country no one
> may construct a building without the permission of
> the government and without being in compliance with
> the plans of government planners.[33]

So impressed is Aminoddowleh with the French that in order to praise them, he finds occasion to compare them with the people and governments of other countries he has visited on his journey. For instance, in contrast to his opinion of the Ottoman Turks who, according to the author, lack the basic rules of hospitality—as he says, in two and a half months of his stay in Istanbul, "none of the people and dignitaries of the Ottoman government invited us to a meal"—Aminoddowleh has abundant praise for French hospitality. France seems to him to be an ideal country governed by peace and tranquility. He compares the French king in his prosperous land to the Prophet Solomon, and on viewing the factories he sees "the talent and capability of human beings."[34]

Although perhaps for political reasons, Aminoddowleh is somewhat partial toward France and the French people in his praise of them, still he is as impressed—and in certain respects more so—by England and the English. In fact, in terms of social services, such as insane asylums and hospitals, he finds the English superior to other Europeans. In praise of them, the author observes:

> Today none of the European governments have the national unity, wealth and commerce, and the stability of the foundations of the government and monarchy as does England. Every building that we observed was like a steel nail driven into stone. The government and the people avoid [excessive] pleasures and epicurism; everyone's attention is focused on the future and on learning the means of building a better life. They are simple in their designs and ornamentation; they have good buildings; and their actions are proper. They do not allow their property to deteriorate.[35]

Further, he observes that the English have planned their endeavors such that:

> Without declaring war, carrying out military expeditions, or killing people, they take control of all the wealth and governments on earth. Every rule and regulation is decided by the government and the people in consultation with one another; and in whatever they build, they try their best to ensure its stability.[36]

The image of Europe presented in *The Treasury of Events* is not merely that of a place to be visited to partake of the pleasures that are not accessible to Iranians in their own country, but of places that have prospered, people who are capable of improving their lives, whose efforts can provide a lesson for Iran and the Iranians of the time to improve their own lot. This can be seen not only in terms of the social and technological advancements of the West, but also in regard to the political systems there. The mere report that "in France, the king and judges cannot issue a death sentence or any other chastisement on their own without adherence to the law and without guilt having been proven" suggests that Aminoddowleh views the European ways as preferable.[37] In the same vein, and with similar intent, he describes an annual ceremony in which the French emperor delivers a speech before the representatives of the people, reporting on the efforts of the government in various industrial, agricultural, educational, and other domestic issues, on the national revenues and expenditures and the relations between France and other countries.[38] Considering that Aminoddowleh was a prominent Iranian government official whose travel diary was to be read by the king and other important personalities in the Iranian ruling elite, there is undoubtedly an implicit lesson to them intended in this *safarnameh*.

Aminoddowleh's admiration for the English and Europeans in general, who looked into the future and thought about creating a better society,reflects his own vision or dreams for a better future for his country, about which he is quite optimistic. Listening to a French merchant who is interested in commerce with Iran and the establishment of a silk-manufacturing factory there, Aminoddowleh is quite impressed by and in agreement with the observations of the merchant, who claims:

Nowadays, it is widely known throughout Europe
that the government of Iran has, in a short period of
time, made as much progress as is possible in fifty
years and, of course, in a short period hence will
regain its status as one of the greatest governments in
the world.[39]

Such optimism should perhaps be expected of a high-ranking official of the Iranian government at the time, who was becoming increasingly aware of the progress in the West compared to the backward conditions in Iran and wished for such advancements in Iran as well. But, awareness of Iran's backwardness in contrast to Europe and the expression of a desire for change is not confined to government officials or dignitaries such as Aminoddowleh. Similar concerns were expressed a decade or two later, for example, by a young, adventurous Iranian in his *Safarnameh-ye Haj Sayyah beh Farang* [The Diary of Haj Sayyah's Travel to Europe].[40]

A young cleric in his early twenties with a sense of adventure, or as he suggests a desire to see and learn about the world, Sayyah embarks on a journey to Europe in the early 1860s via Russia (the most common route for Iranian travelers to the West at that time). Unlike the previous travelers discussed, he begins his journey with no specific destination in mind and lacking the financial means required for extended travel. In fact, he sets out on foot with only the clerical garb he is wearing. The paltry sum of money that he has in his pocket is exhausted even before he leaves his own country, and for the remainder of his journey, he surrenders himself to fate. Nevertheless, despite hardships, thanks to the kindness of strangers along the way, he manages to travel for a period of several years throughout most of Europe.

Sayyah is most impressed by the fact that in every place he has visited, people and governments pay attention to the education of children; he also remarks on how informed the Westerners with whom he comes in contact are about the world. He is amazed at the wonders of Europe and envies the Europeans, but he still sees education as the basis for this progress. On his way to Italy, walking in the countryside, he is invited by a small family of farmers to spend the night. Since the family is poor and their house small, he must spend the night in the bedroom of their twelve-year-old son. He describes the simple furnishings of the room, "a clock on the wall; two tables, one for writing and another for washing; a bookshelf on which books were arranged. On the other side was a bed. A few nails in the wall for hanging clothes and hat ... with a candle on the child's desk." He then describes the activities of the boy, who changes his clothes as soon as he returns from school and begins to study. Later, he finishes some chores, such as feeding the animals. And finally, every night after supper, all the members of the family "study books on history, ethics, industry, and agriculture." Comparing this way of life with that of his own country, he writes, "I was so saddened: Why should our country not have such education and our people be so uninformed?"[41]

Sayyah's preoccupation with the education of children is often verbalized in his answer to those who ask him his purpose in traveling, to which he generally responds that he would like to inform the people of his country about the rest of the world. But although the general image that he provides of the West is quite positive—in England, for instance, he states, "We must learn humanity and foresight from these people"[42]—he is on occasion quite critical of the West. In Brussels, he is told by the Belgian king that everything in Europe is better than in Asia, to which he responds that although the king is certainly correct, the people of Asia are, however, greatly apprehensive of some of the European industries, especially the weapons industry. He adds that the Asians do not understand the European attitude toward killing, that the Asian community maintains, "We try our best to even eliminate the sword so that there will be no instruments of killing left"; yet, compared with the wars of the past, the wars that were fought with the sword alone, in which only a small number of people were killed, those of the present day are horrendous. Even so, he asserts, lamenting, "Now, the Europeans try their best to advance the instruments of killing, so that on one day alone a hundred thousand people or even more are killed."[43]

Interestingly, in Haj Sayyah's observations about the West and Westerners, he rarely deals with European customs and beliefs. On the occasion when he does—as when, for instance, he notices antagonism toward priests in Italy—he merely reports quite impartially what he has observed. Surprisingly, despite his religious upbringing and background, he does not appear to be offended or shocked, as many secular Iranian travelers were, by the degree of relative freedom, particularly in terms of dress and social behavior, that European societies allow women. In this respect, as well, Sayyah displays a positive view of Western society and seems to approve of emulation of the West.

This optimism, however, is not thoroughly shared by many other Iranians who traveled to Europe in the late nineteenth century. One such traveler is Haji Pirzadeh, a Sufi elder who gained prominence as a spiritual leader among the elite and the general public during the Qajar period.

Haji Pirzadeh, who had visited Europe nearly two decades earlier, travels to Europe once again in the mid-1880s, visiting France, England, Germany, and Austria.[44] Like Sayyah, he is not on an official visit, but, being more advanced in age and more experienced about the world, he pays close attention to those aspects of European society that are either neglected or dealt with only in passing by earlier travelers.

Like other Iranian travelers to the West, Haji Pirzadeh is awed by Western progress. Describing the avenues and boulevards of Paris, he is quite fascinated with how the streets are paved, with the sidewalks for pedestrians, with the signs indicating street names, with the benches placed in various spots for resting, with how clean everything is kept, with how trees are planted to provide shade, and with how the streets are lit at night. In short, he writes, "all avenues and streets in Paris are so pleasant, clean, and filled with trees and lights, as if every avenue and street were made for a king and cleaned every hour of every day in expectation of the king walking by."[45] He is impressed by the postal system, the buildings, and the factories, on the whole, by the affluence of the people. Europe, he writes, is a prosperous place with remarkable buildings and pleasant dwellings, adding:

> There is an abundant means of pleasure, all sorts of
> comfort. People live in such comfort and affluence
> that the poor cannot be distinguished from the rich.
> All people wear expensive clothes made of silk and
> broadcloth, adorned with jewelry. Every home and
> building is like a royal palace. Gardens and orchards
> in the city and outside the city are like Paradise, and
> homes are furnished in luxury that is indescribable.
> ... They have created all sorts of parks, forests, and
> artificial lakes in the countryside, where people go on
> excursions in carriages ... and do not allow any
> sadness or sorrow to enter their hearts. The means
> for a comfortable life is provided for them; their
> income is secure, and they know what their expenses
> will be; and their wealth is abundant. They do what
> they please and go where they please. They can say
> what they wish and buy whatever they see.[46]

In short, the picture that he presents in this and similar passages is utopian. The author begins to realize, however, that this paradise belongs for the most part to the rich and the aristocracy, who walk in parks hand in hand "as if each and every man is the king of a country and each and every woman the wife of a king ... as if divine blessing, joys, and pleasures

were created for them alone."[47]   On the other hand, he learns,
there are also those who "drown themselves in the river because
of destitution and poverty."[48]   As his sense of wonderment
subsides and he begins to see beyond the superficial glamor of
this new culture, given Haji Pirzadeh's background as a spiritual
leader, his criticism of European society is directed most often
against the moral corruption that he observes, particularly in
French society.   After describing public dances held in various
parts of Paris, for instance, he comments:

> Such parties are organized so that anyone who wants
> a woman or a lover, even a woman who wants to
> have a lover, can find one by attending them.   There
> are many such gatherings in Paris.   For this reason,
> there is not a chaste woman to be found in Paris who
> would preserve herself.[49]

Further on, after describing detailed examples of various
types of entertainment in Paris, such as theaters, circuses, and
cabarets, he writes:

> In any case, plays and theater in Paris are all of this
> kind, by which they have robbed the people of their
> thinking faculties.   After work, people spend most of
> their time watching such comedies and plays.
> Religion, faith, spirituality, truth, humanity, chastity,
> chivalry, and honor can by no means be found.
> What is widespread is absolute ignorance,
> superficiality, appearances, perdition, depravity, and
> aberration.   May God protect any human being from
> such places, save the followers of Islam from coming
> to this land, and [protect] Moslems from dying in
> such places.[50]

As for the religious side of Parisians, he states: "Some Parisians
go to church routinely on Sundays and perform prayers, as is
their custom.   But this is merely a convention, rather than
worshipping."[51]   Even though Europeans live a life of comfort
and luxury, and Haji Pirzadeh describes their affluent life with
a degree of envy, he is concerned about his fellow compatriots
being exposed to European life and beliefs, and not without
reason.   Apparently having observed the behavior of an
increasing number of Iranian students in Paris, he comments:

> May God have mercy on some of the young people of
> our Iran who come here [to Europe] and to Paris and
> who upon seeing the superficial glitter of Paris
> suddenly lose themselves, abandon their religion,
> beliefs, purity, cleanliness, piety, true worship, and
> religiousness and become confused and bewildered.
> They do not know what they must do. They think
> that if they drink wine, eat pork and crab, refrain
> from washing themselves after bowel movements,
> refuse to pray, and reject speaking the truth, they
> shall gain wealth and status, like the Europeans.
> May God curse such people, because one Iranian of
> this kind in the West will destroy the reputation of
> the entire nation.[52]

He further worries that "the Westerners will think that all
Iranians are irreligious and weak in their beliefs, that as soon as
they enter a European city, they lose their religion, laws, and
tradition and pollute themselves with any sort of debauchery."[53]

For the most part, Haji Pirzadeh's attitude toward the West
and Westerners can be described as ambivalent. On the one
hand, he explains rather approvingly that before marriage, boys
and girls associate with each other and become familiar with
each other's characters. He also seems to approve of their
independence in choosing their spouse, even in the case of girls,
whose parents "cannot dictate to them" and who may "marry
anyone they wish."[54] Yet, on the other hand, he disapproves of
the freedom that Paris affords women, most of whom he
describes as prostitutes. "The truth is," he writes, "that this
freedom is, in fact, lewdness and lack of chastity." He goes on
to add with regard to married women:

> No one can control his wife in that city. If a woman
> so wishes, she is free to go with any man, even a
> stranger. Her husband cannot protest and prevent
> her, because that woman is free, and Europe is the
> land of freedom. Hence, the meaning of freedom
> must be merely the woman's choice to be unchaste;
> otherwise, in the West, the people are not free at
> all.[55]

The warning of Haji Pirzadeh against young Iranians being
sent to Europe obviously had its foundation in his disapproval

of the immorality that he saw in the European societies.   But
there were also those, particularly Qajar government officials,
who warned against traveling to and knowing about the West
for political reasons.   For instance, Mirza Aqa Khan Nuri, the
grand minister of Naseroddin Shah, had warned Farrokh Khan
Aminoddowleh against publishing his travel diary, *The Treasury
of Events*, because "if this book is published and distributed
everywhere, the people will learn the truth about the conditions
of Europe, which is not in [our] best interests."[56]   On the
whole, however, these warnings, particularly those of the latter
sort, went unheeded.   Naseroddin Shah himself made three visits
to Europe, the first in 1873.

In the last decade of the nineteenth century, travel diaries
still remained in the category of books of wonders about strange
lands and people.   Nevertheless, a greater degree of
understanding and knowledge about the West and Westerners is
exhibited by these travelers. *Safarnameh-ye Shikago* [The Diary of
Travel to Chicago] by Haj Mirza Mohammad Ali Mo'inossaltaneh
is a prime example.[57]

Mo'inossaltaneh's main purpose is to attend the 1893
Chicago World's Columbian Exposition and at the same time
tour the United States.   He had earlier visited the 1889 Paris
Exposition and was, therefore, more aware of what to expect
than many other writers of travel diaries.   At the same time,
unlike Haj Sayyah, for instance, he seems unconcerned about
expenses, since he is a member of an affluent merchant family.
The glitter of Europe does not seem to impress this traveler as
much as it had his predecessors; even so, he is keenly aware of
the new inventions in the West that are still unavailable in his
own country.   Being a practical man, when he describes a
building or an invention, he provides minute details, even down
to the cost, as if intending to reproduce it once back home.   Of
particular interest are Mo'inossaltaneh's observations of the lands
and people on the two sides of the Atlantic, particularly his
characterizations of Americans and America in the late
nineteenth century.

On the whole, Mo'inossaltaneh displays an ambivalent
outlook toward Americans and their society.   On the one hand,
he praises the Americans for their innovations and industries
and implicitly approves of their system of government, their
sense of equality, and their self-reliance.   For instance, he
comments on the fact that the people are allowed two days a
week to visit the president, who listens to their complaints and

other concerns. He is also impressed by various museums and other public buildings which have been built with donations from the people. On the other hand, his comments about the people and their behavior are often contemptuous. In New York, he finds the people to be "very able-bodied and rough, [and] much freer than the Europeans," but, he adds, "their barbarians are also more barbaric than European barbarians."[58] In Philadelphia, he finds the children "very impolite and uncivilized; they explode firecrackers near the horses pulling carts and spook them so they run away."[59] In a public park, listening to a band, he comments that he does not "dare to walk ten steps away [from where the band is playing]." He claims: "The people here are not civilized. But for a few, the rest are savages. A person fears for his life should he wish to walk to a quiet corner of the park."[60] Further, he observes that "the people of this city want to imitate the Europeans, but it is clear that they are impolite by nature." Nevertheless, the one city that truly impresses this traveler is San Francisco, which he describes as a "city so beautiful and clean, the likes of which I have never seen before," with "people who are proficient and experienced and quite different from other people in America. They have a strong desire to imitate the Europeans and behave like them. But at the same time, they do not follow the typical customs and traditions of the Europeans."[61] These impressions notwithstanding, it is only after leaving America, on his way home through Europe, that Mo'inossaltaneh notes that not even Paris compares with the United States. He writes: "It is amazing that now that I have returned from America to Europe, Paris and London and their buildings and theaters do not seem to be as interesting and beautiful as they did before."[62]

Another traveler to Europe and the United States in the late nineteenth century is Ebrahim Sahhafbashi. Apparently a businessman, Sahhafbashi was an experienced traveler who had visited these places on numerous occasions within the twenty years prior to this journey. Early in his travel diary, he comments on other *safarnameh*s written by Iranians about the West:

> Most of my compatriots who go to the West see the
> conditions of the Westerners, and then they have a
> flight of imagination and decide to step into the
> realm of hyperbole. Once they return home, after a
> while, they become unpaid liars. The ideas of the

Westerners are a mix of good and bad. Obviously, to
some extent they are right. On the surface, they go
around quite clean. But they eat like animals and
they roar. If they sit next to one another on a bench
for ten days, they pay no attention to each other.
They wait for someone else to appear and introduce
them to each other, whereas just saying hello is itself
an introduction.[63]

Sahhafbashi's efforts in his travel diary to set the record straight,
as it were, indicate that traveling to the West had become a
relatively common practice for many Iranians who were not
necessarily very rich but financially comfortable. In Paris, after
spending a day visiting the Eiffel Tower, he calculates his
expenses for the day, which add up to twenty tomans (forty
dollars at the time), and records, not without some degree of
humor:

My purpose in writing all this is to show that if our
friends [compatriots] have a thousand tomans [$2,000],
they should not long to go to Europe and imagine
buying all sorts of souvenirs. Everyone who has
written a travel diary has written nothing but praise,
which has made all those who have heard [read] it
develop a yearning for it [the West]. In any case, the
West is nothing special, except for its lights and good
streets. Its houses are like cages, with no room to
breathe. And their food is bad and expensive. Those
who wish to see the West should light up a myriad
of lamps, rent countless dishes, and look at a
landscape painting through a magnifying glass and
keep the rest of the money in their own pockets!
What they will see is just like Europe. Were it not
for business, I would never come to Europe to eat
dog meat and spend two or three thousand tomans to
live like a beggar.[64]

But despite his warnings to his compatriots who might
harbor the wish to visit Europe and the United States, this
traveler, too, finds much worthy of praise in the West. In
particular, Western agriculture and industry, political freedom,
social services, education, and the involvement of women in
social life are aspects of the West that Sahhafbashi describes with

approval. "One of the good characteristics of the Westerners," he writes, "is that if you ask them something they do not know, they consult a book, and if they do not find it, they ask another person. Even if they have to spend half an hour, they give you the correct answer."[65] He is likewise impressed by the rule of law in Europe, where "people do not bother each other, even when they are drunk." At the same time, his descriptions of life in large cities imply an awareness of the social problems emergent in industrialized Europe at the turn of the century, particularly prostitution. With regard to the United States, on the other hand, despite his occasional complaint about high prices, Sahhafbashi presents a more positive image than that of Europe. He finds Americans wealthier and freer, the cities more organized, and the people more honest and hard working. "In a short period of time," he writes, "they have built cities that would require hundreds of years to build—good for them!"[66] Old and young alike are active, he writes, adding, "I never saw an old woman or an old man walk panting with a cane or complain about his miserable life."[67]

The travel diary of Sahhafbashi is particularly interesting since it offers a more dispassionate description of the West and Westerners from the perspective of a relatively well-informed Iranian and in some ways foreshadows the attitudes of many Iranian writers in the century about to begin. Although Sahhafbashi's observations were undoubtedly affected by the impressions of his predecessors, whose works, as witnessed in the examples in this chapter, included both positive and negative images of the West and Westerners, his portrayal of the West and Westerners is neither totally positive nor fully negative. Rather, the images are mixed. This ambivalent attitude permeates not only later travel diaries, even as late as the 1960s and 1970s, but is interwoven in the works which are the subject of the following chapters, in Iranian prose fiction.[68]

One notable feature of the travel diaries discussed is how virtually every traveler is intensely awed and fascinated by Western technological advancements. Literally hundreds of pages in nearly every *safarnameh* are devoted to descriptions of factories, agricultural innovations, architectural advancements, and various inventions. These travelers view these signs of Western progress with envy, even covetousness, and, at the same time, inquisitiveness as to how such technology can be developed in or transported to Iran. With respect to technological advancements, they express admiration for the West and praise Westerners for their achievements.

A second observation common among these travelers concerns government, or more specifically, what they viewed as a democratic system of government. Most accounts avoid any direct comparison between Iranian and European or American forms of government, which is understandable, given that their travel diaries were written to be read in Iran and they would most likely have faced repercussions if they had commented negatively on their own government. Nonetheless, often the mere description of, for example, the responsibilities of the French king vis-à-vis the people and how he is accountable before the Parliament in his operation of the country clearly indicates the writer's partiality toward the Western forms and implies criticism of the Iranian government.

Another intense source of interest with regard to the West for these travelers, particularly those in government service, relates to military matters, in terms not only of new weaponry, but of the orderliness and discipline of soldiers, and even their uniforms.[69] This interest is understandable in light of the awareness on the part of nineteenth-century Iranians of their comparative weakness and vulnerability, considering the military superiority of the Western powers. Many travelers devote numerous pages to detailed descriptions of European barracks, military hospitals, weapons, and so on, as if to suggest that exact duplication of these facilities would help Iran regain its former position of power and distinction in the world.

In addition, these travelers were preoccupied by the provision of social services in the European societies, such as asylums for the mentally ill; paved and lighted streets and public parks; and the attention paid to the education of children; not to mention being absorbed with detailed descriptions of entertainment and the arts, particularly the theater, operas, and museums.[70]

The features mentioned above are among the positive aspects of the West admired by early Iranian travelers who unabashedly wished Iran to emulate them. However, other aspects of the West and Westerners toward which they displayed a negative or at best an ambivalent attitude are also noteworthy.

The attitudes of most writers of travel diaries toward European women, for example, fall into this category. On the one hand, they view European and American women working in factories and shops as a positive phenomenon. On the other hand, however, they judge European women to be loose in their behavior and morals. These writers also look negatively on the manner of dress of European women, particularly in formal gatherings, such as dances and the theater. Obviously making judgments based on the value system of their own society, many comment on the way women "display" their naked shoulders and breasts.

In a similar vein, accounts of the relations between men and women abound. At times, these visitors to the West approve of the freedom that they detect permeating the relationship between men and women. But often, sometimes in the same breath, they feel that such freedom has made Paris, for instance, a city of prostitutes, where every young girl and woman, so it seems to them, is only waiting for a man, longing to be picked up by any man. They view most dances and even evening walks in the lighted streets or parks as serving this purpose.

The emphasis placed by Europeans on entertainment and living the good life also leaves these Iranian travelers with mixed emotions regarding them. Even though they appear envious of the way Westerners enjoy their lives, they also find in Western societies a decided lack of spirituality.[71]

Among the negative impressions of the West made on these travelers are those resulting from their confrontations with swindlers who try to dupe them. In this respect, some writers comment that parallel with technological and social progress, Westerners have also made advancements in charlatanism.[72] Many of these travelers also comment negatively on the price which they feel is put on human kindness. For instance, several travelers comment on restaurants, with which they have been delighted in terms of the service and hospitality they received, only to realize upon their departure that such hospitality is commensurate with the price they have been charged.[73]

One important feature of these travel diaries is, of course, the generally negative attitude of Iranians, for political reasons, toward particular Western countries. For the most part, the British and the Russians are regarded with suspicion, due no doubt to their visible involvement in the affairs of Iran at the time.

In sum, the accounts of the West and Westerners provided by these travelers appear weighted on the positive side. Western progress in social, economic, and technological matters by comparison to the stagnant conditions in Iran provided sufficient evidence to support advocating emulation of Western ways. Democratic ideas found their way into the Constitutional

Revolution of 1906–1911, and many notable Iranians at that time advocated the restructuring and overhauling of Iranian society on the basis of Western models. But at the same time, others regarded such emulation with a degree of apprehension, and exhibited a more conservative attitude toward the changes that were advocated and eventually implemented.

As a genre, the *safarnameh* tends to be a hybrid of fact and fiction, the writers attempting, on the one hand, to record an account of the places they visit, things they see and people they meet, and on the other, making observations or expressing personal opinions, thus providing the reader with their own view of their encounters. Even though the intention of these authors is to leave the reader with the impression that they are objective in their presentation of their views of places, people, and customs with which the reader is unfamiliar, they betray both overt and implicit subjectivity with regard to their experiences, which is further enhanced by the fact that the writers of travel diaries also often focus selectively on the exotic and may resort to exaggerations and even inventions to make their work more interesting and appealing to the reader. In effect, *safarnameh*s, particularly those dealing with the West, can arguably be studied as fictional or semifictional reconstructions of the West. In other words, the author of a travel diary becomes a creative artist to some extent, mixing fact and fiction or writing a sort of documentary fiction. In this light, the personality, background, education, social status, upbringing, and attitudes of the author become an inseparable part of the narrative. Indeed, the narrative "I" becomes a fictional character and usually the protagonist of a story of travel adventure. This becomes particularly evident and at the same time technically more complex in the case of *safarnameh*s which have been written by professional scribes accompanying a dignitary for the sole purpose of writing the travel diary. In such cases the scribe functions, in fact, as the author and the dignitary as a perceived character in the story, albeit one created on the basis of an actual person.[74]

The writers of *safarnameh*s were at least to some extent aware of the fictional dimension of their endeavor, and fictional works such as *Siyahatnameh-ye Ebrahim Beyg* [*The Travel Diary of Ebrahim Beyg*], discussed in the following chapter, functioned as a bridge between the genre of the *safarnameh* and modern fiction.

As the following chapters intend to show, many of the impressions left on nineteenth-century Iranian travelers by

Western societies and Westerners prevail in twentieth-century fiction.   The images of the West and Westerners presented by Iranian novelists and short-story writers may at times be as stereotypical as those given by the writers of the travel diaries, although rather complex and sophisticated portrayals of the West and Westerners are also evident.   In either case, such portraits often function for the Iranian reader as an image for comparison.

3

THE WEST IN CONTRAST

Of the various historical forces that influenced the social and political changes in Iran in the first decade of the twentieth century and which were manifested in the Constitutional Revolution (1906–1911), increasing exposure to the West undoubtedly played a significant role.[1] As was discussed in the previous chapter, Iranian travelers to Europe and America initially viewed the West as a land of marvels and wrote their travel diaries as books of wonders, often choosing to depict aspects of the West and Westerners that would seem rather strange to Iranians, which inevitably functioned to emphasize and even magnify the dichotomy between the Self and the Other. Nevertheless, the increasing knowledge of Iranians about the West and Western societies gradually opened their eyes to not only the scientific and technological advancements but also the social and political progress of the West, particularly when juxtaposed with the seemingly stagnant and backward conditions evident in their own country. Such ultimate comparisons, whether implicit or explicit, also led to a certain sense of self-consciousness. Many Iranian intellectuals began to use their understanding of the West as a touchstone with which to evaluate and ultimately criticize their own society and its political, religious, and other institutions. Hence, the travel diaries may have served and, at least for some Iranians, came to be viewed as a vehicle for the expression of their discontent with existing conditions in Iran at the time. It is perhaps for this reason that one of the earliest works of modern Persian prose fiction, *Siyahatnameh-ye Ebrahim Beyg* [*The Travel Diary of Ebrahim Beyg*], was conceived and written by Zeynol'abedin Maragheh'i in the form of a travel diary.[2]

The Travel Diary of Ebrahim Beyg, the first volume of which was published in 1895 in Cairo, is the story of Ebrahim, an

Iranian born and reared in Egypt, and his visit to Iran in the
latter part of the nineteenth century. Ebrahim's father, who was
a wealthy merchant, had a great devotion to the country of his
birth. Although the father had spent many years away from his
homeland, his love for his native country was so strong that he
could not tolerate any criticism of it on the part of anyone. In
his son, too, he instilled this fanatical passion for Iran. He had
told his son before dying:

> Never lose your good national customs. Some
> dishonorable individuals speak ill of Iran; do not
> believe them. These are all lies. Even if they happen
> to tell the truth about all of this, do not join them in
> speaking ill of your homeland.[3]

The son's excessive yearning to see his fatherland is
sufficient to launch him on a journey to Iran, where, contrary to
his expectations, he finds a country in ruins, most of whose
people live in poverty, where conditions are ever so much worse
than he had been told by its detractors. He finds Iran to be a
land permeated with corruption, from the lowest to the highest
official, where government and religious leaders alike thrive on
the misery of the people, and no one seems even remotely
concerned about improving conditions. He sums up his
impressions of Iran as follows:

> What does not exist [in Iran] is law. There is no
> order. For this reason, no one's duty, including that
> of the rulers and the subjects, the peasants and the
> officials, is clear. Hence, it has no schools and no
> taxes, but it does have bribery, dictatorship and
> extortion. Cities are left in ruins; farms are
> abandoned uncultivated; waters have become
> stagnant, such that one cannot pass through the
> streets without being overcome by their stench.
> Beggars have become ministers and ministers have
> become beggars. The affairs have fallen into the
> hands of the incompetent. All that exists are
> swindling, exploitation, and chaos.[4]

The author of *The Travel Diary of Ebrahim Beyg*, who like his
protagonist had spent most of his life outside Iran, was relatively
familiar with the progress made in Western countries. Like the

writers of travel diaries on visits to the West, he also takes
advantage of various opportunities to report on the progress
made in Europe and to juxtapose it with the conditions that
Ebrahim observes and describes in Iran. On the benefits of the
press and the ability of Westerners to criticize themselves, he
writes:

> Today, it is obvious to everyone that the major reason
> behind the progress of the Western nations is the
> press in those fortunate countries, which publishes for
> the public in their newspapers all the deficiencies
> found in their countries, concerning any class in the
> society or any branch of the government, as they see
> or hear, once they are absolutely certain of what they
> have seen and heard, without any personal
> considerations or selfish intentions, thereby reminding
> the officials to rectify those deficiencies. Any
> responsible official, too, as soon as he is reminded by
> the press, without wasting a minute, takes steps to
> investigate the deficiencies. If the claim of the press
> is true, he immediately begins to set things right and
> even thanks the critic. And if no transgression has
> occurred, he politely points out that a mistake in
> reporting has been made. Hence, it can be said that
> the fortunate citizens of those domains possess a
> tongue that speaks, eyes that see, and ears that hear.
> Unfortunately, we are deprived of all three.[5]

Unaccustomed to the behavior of Iranian rulers toward their
subjects, Ebrahim Beyg is shocked to see the submissive reaction
of the populace to the governor of a small province. The young
governor, riding through the city, is preceded by thirty or forty
guards armed with clubs, who beat the people and force them
to bow to the governor as he passes by. Ebrahim Beyg writes
sarcastically:

> Because I had never seen a situation such as this
> anywhere else, I was astounded. I said to myself,
> "Bless you, Iran!" When the ruler of a city like
> London, with a population of seven million, walks
> anywhere, no one pays any attention to him. Yet, the
> governor of one of our small provinces, may God
> protect him, enjoys such pomp and circumstance.

Now this is the way to govern![6]

As for cities, he compares, for example, Qazvin to European cities and states:

> This city of Qazvin was once the capital but has now
> lost its luster. It is very filthy and is in ruins.
> Compared to the cities of the West, it cannot even be
> considered a village, because in Europe, even the
> doors and walls in the cities seem to have a soul and
> feelings. One can see how they thrive in business
> when one sees how the people come and go in large
> numbers and how they are engaged in transactions.
> You cannot even find one person unemployed in the
> whole city. Everyone works and tries to increase the
> national wealth and make his country prosper. By
> way of contrast, in Iran, no matter where you look,
> there are idle, unemployed people sitting around in
> droves. The cities are all in ruins and are like
> graveyards.[7]

Upon visiting a town ravaged by a smallpox epidemic, in response to a cleric who considers the death of hundreds of children and the blindness of many to be the will of God, he says:

> Today, Germany has a population of fifty million. In
> the entire country of Germany, six hundred children
> do not die of smallpox in one whole year. But out of
> extreme laziness, ignorance and lack of awareness, in
> this small town alone you have annihilated seven
> hundred innocent children who are the main
> foundation of the nation's future population, and you
> blame it on the will of God.[8]

Maragheh'i's implicit praise of the West and Westerners is most evident in the observations of his protagonist, when his intention is to point out the shortcomings of Iranians and their society to them. But at the same time, interestingly, in his dealing with the relationship between the Iranian government and the Western powers of the time, Ebrahim's commentary reveals the author's negative impression of European governments, particularly those of the English and the French.

On one occasion, for instance, Ebrahim eavesdrops on a conversation between an Englishman and a young Iranian and finds out that the Englishman, who is an agent of a British company, has bribed the prime minister, and perhaps the king, into granting him mining concessions in Iran. In other words, the image that Maragheh'i presents of the Westerners is positive with regard to Western progress, but negative as it concerns Western exploitation of Iran.

The presentation of aspects of the West for the purpose of pointing out the social problems of Iran continued into the early decades of the twentieth century. An example is a short story called "Bileh Dig Bileh Choghondar" [translated into English as "What's Sauce for the Goose ..."], included in Mohammad Ali Jamalzadeh's pioneering collection, *Yeki Bud, Yeki Nabud* (1921) [translated as *Once upon a Time*].[9] In this story, the author employs a Western character to explicitly criticize Iranian social institutions.

Jamalzadeh utilizes an anecdotal format to tell the story of a European masseur who accompanies his employer, a European advisor invited to Iran by the government. The main purpose in the masseur's visit to Iran is to render his services to his master, who has been suffering physical pain. Unwilling to pay for the travel and living expenses of the masseur out of his own pocket, the "master" decides to keep the professional identity of the masseur a secret and passes him off to the Iranian officials as a member of his advisory team. Once in Iran, in his new capacity, the masseur is put in charge of reforming the postal system and eventually becomes a consultant to several ministries. Relying on his own common sense, the masseur becomes even more successful than his master and begins to accumulate some degree of wealth. Eventually, however, fearing that his good fortune may be fleeting, he decides to return to Europe. But his attempt to bring with him the wealth he has accumulated fails, since he is robbed by a gang of bandits. Back home, he is obliged to resume his profession as a masseur, but later writes a travel diary of sorts dealing with Iranian government and religious institutions as well as various kinds of people.

The anecdote of the masseur combined with the travel notes is a device used by Jamalzadeh to indirectly voice his criticism of the Iranian society of the time through the eyes of a Westerner, as it were.[10] The West and Westerners in the story are not directly targets of blame for the ills and mismanagement of the Iranian society. And even though the masseur is portrayed as a naive European, the West and Westerners implicitly provide a contrast to Iran and Iranians, which are the main targets of criticism in the story.

On the situation of women in Iran, for example, Jamalzadeh's criticism is indirect. The masseur comments in his travel notes: "One strange thing about this country is that, apparently, there are absolutely no women in it. You see little girls, four or five years old, in the alleyways but never any women."[11] Women, of course, the reader soon recognizes from the further comments of the masseur, are not actually absent from the Iranian society, but appear in public in full body-length veils. The masseur writes:

> Another thing that is very strange about Iran is that a
> substantial part of the people, about half the
> population of the country, wrap themselves from
> head to foot in black sacks, not even leaving a space
> to breathe. And that's how they go about the
> alleyways, in that black sack. These people are never
> allowed to speak and have no right to enter a
> teahouse or any other place. Their baths are also
> separate and, at public gatherings like passion plays
> and mourning-fests, they have their own viewing
> sections. As long as they are alone, you never hear a
> peep from them, but as soon as they get together,
> they start cackling weirdly. I believe they are a form
> of Iranian priest, similar to the strange types of
> priests we have back home in Europe. If they are
> indeed priests, the people do not seem to hold them
> in much respect, for they have dubbed them *zaifeh*,
> which means "weak" and "insignificant."[12]

In regard to social stratification, Jamalzadeh presents his compatriots with a picture that appears as strange as that of the women of the society. The masseur comments that the men in Iran are distinguished by their hats and consist of three basic groups: The Yellow Hats, the White Hats, and the Black Hats. The reader learns later that these groups represent the peasants, the clerics, and the government officials, respectively. The Western observer is puzzled as to why the Yellow Hats, who "enjoy complete equality in their poverty and want and in even their demise," sacrifice their "belongings, their honor and reputation, and even their souls and those of their family" to the other two classes.[13]   The masseur writes:

> I don't know why they have vowed to work as hard
> as they can all their lives and to present the other
> two groups, the White Hats and the Black Hats, with
> the fruits of their labor.   They are so insistent upon
> this that often both they themselves and their families
> starve to death or die from the cold and are buried
> without so much as a shroud, while the Black Hats
> and the White Hats have profited so much from the
> Yellow Hats' suffering that they have no idea how to
> spend their money.[14]

Jamalzadeh's stories, generally speaking, deal with traditional Iranian society and are viewed in particular by many critics as recreations of a bygone era, roughly at the turn of the century, when Jamalzadeh left Iran.[15]   His having lived in Europe nearly all his life and, therefore, his intimate knowledge of the West have inevitably resulted in the creation of many Western characters and comments about the West in his work, but not without purpose.   In other words, Jamalzadeh customarily uses the West and Westerners in his fiction, as in the story cited above, to instruct his countrymen on how to improve their own society.

Another writer who also began his career in the early decades of the twentieth century is Sadeq Hedayat (1903–1951), perhaps the best known fiction writer in Iran.   Like Jamalzadeh, Hedayat had extensive experience living in Europe and created numerous Western characters in his stories.   Also like Jamalzadeh, his employment of the West and Western characters was intended, whether directly or indirectly, to juxtapose those aspects of Iranian society of which he disapproved with aspects of Western society.   This is essentially true both of his satirical writings and his more somber works.

In *Karvan-e Eslam: Al-Be'sat ol-Eslamiyyah ela al-Belad al-Faranjiyyah* [The Caravan of Islam: The Islamic Mission to European Countries], Hedayat casts a satirical glance at the perception of the West by clerics and, on the whole, Moslem religious fanatics.[16]   Presented in the form of three reports prepared by a journalist for the fictional *Al-Manjelab* [The Cesspool] magazine, the story relates the activities of the missionary group.   The first report is on a meeting between several clerics from various Islamic countries on propagating the faith in Europe. America is exempted as a missionary target, because in America, assures one of the participants, the people "have recently learned about the philosophy of Islam," as they have "put a prohibition on alcoholic beverages," and, among other things, their philosophers and learned men have come to the conclusion that "circumcision is very beneficial to health," along with divorce, polygamy, and fasting.[17] Hence, the only place remaining in which people still are unenlightened and have not converted to Islam is Europe. For this reason the religious scholars, who are "the guardians of the foundations of religion," find it their duty to select a number of people from among themselves to dispatch to the lands of the "infidels" in order to guide the people away from the deviant path to the path of truth, and to uproot unbelief and heathenism.[18]

The attitude of Hedayat's religious characters toward the West and Westerners is based on a parody of the traditional views of Moslems who consider the West as *dar al-harb* [the abode of war].[19] To these characters, who represent the closed-minded and superstitious clergy, it is no longer a philosophical or theological belief that forms their perception of the "land of the infidels," but, instead, popular lore and tales about the West. "The women of the infidels," reports a member of the assembly, "dance with their naked bodies exposed in public, with men, and commit tribadism and flirtation."[20] Further on, the assembly is informed that the people of Europe "eat crabs, lobsters, frogs, and pigs," for they might otherwise starve to death.[21]

The missionaries finally arrive in Europe, where their exotic dress and behavior attract the attention of the public, who take them for a group of oriental showmen. Film companies, circuses and zoos vie to employ them, and they are eventually put on display at a zoo with a sign reading "Oriental Exhibition."

Two and a half years following the arrival of the Islamic missionaries in Europe, the correspondent of the Arabic magazine finds them in Paris. To his astonishment, the missionaries have become quite Europeanized and are living happily in Paris holding such odd jobs as cardsharp, pimp, and tavern keeper. When the reporter asks them about their previous beliefs and zeal for Islam, one of the missionaries responds that Islam is based on two principles, the sword and the begging hand, and that, furthermore, the paradise that Islam promises, in which a Moslem man is given a beautiful angel in addition to such amenities as a large palace, cannot be compared to the paradise they have found in Europe with the beautiful

European girls. In fact, this same missionary observes that he would give up the promised Islamic paradise for the hell where all these beautiful women of Europe are supposed to go.[22]

The target of Hedayat's biting satire is, of course, the clergy. To many Iranian readers, his mocking representation of the perceptions and attitudes of this group is quite realistic and unexaggerated. But, given Hedayat's anti-Islamic attitude, his satire is also indirectly pointed toward those European scholars who praise Islam.[23] In response to the reporter's question, "Have so many European philosophers and scholars not written books in praise of Islam?" the former missionary says:

> That, too, is in line with the colonialist policy [of the West]. These books are written under instructions to control and better dominate us Easterners. What poison, what opiate could make the people more lethargic, strip them of talent and corrupt their morals than the philosophy of fate and destiny held by the Jews and Moslems? Take a look at a world map. You can see that all the Islamic nations are suppressed, comprised of miserable spies, puppets and mercenaries. In order to appease them or create disunity among Hindus and Moslems, the colonialist countries pay cash to these greedy writers to write such utter nonsense.[24]

The portrait of Westerners and the general attitude of Iranians, particularly from a traditional religious point of view, toward the West in this story by Hedayat is indirect and to some extent impersonal. But at the same time, while the initial segment of the story is a parody of the traditional attitudes of the clergy and religious Iranians toward the West, the passage quoted describes the frame of mind of many educated Iranians, particularly since the early twentieth century, who considered Islam, indeed religion in general, to be an obstacle to progress and hence perceived the attention of Western Orientalist and other scholars to Islam to be a part of an overall plot by colonialist powers to subjugate weaker nations such as Iran.[25]

Whether or not Hedayat himself subscribed to this characterization of the West and Westerners is a matter of conjecture. However, this type of portrayal of Westerners is, on the whole, found in his satirical writing, in which in the context of ridiculing the traditional beliefs, superstitions, and practices of his compatriots he also finds occasion for satirizing the West and Westerners. The most famous example is *Tup-e Morvari* [The Pearl Cannon], a raillery of Iranian superstitious beliefs and Iranian history, but also of that of the West, including Christopher Columbus and the discovery of the New World.[26]

Given the fact that Hedayat had spent a significant part of his life in Europe, as well as his familiarity with the West, it is not surprising that his more serious work includes Western characters who are not portrayed as caricatures, but individuals, in whom he invests the intellectual and emotional depth that he employs in his more memorable Iranian fictional persona. In fact, in many of these instances, his treatment of his Western characters appears to be more sympathetic than that of the Iranian characters in his stories.

In "Takht-e Abu Nasr" [The Throne of Abu Nasr] (1942), for example, a team of archaeologists from the Chicago Metropolitan Museum is exploring an ancient site in southern Iran.[27] Dr. Warner and his two assistants, Gorest and Freeman, discover the mummified remains of an ancient king along with instructions to bring the mummy back to life. Although the subject of the story seems ripe for a satirist like Hedayat to launch an attack on superstitious beliefs, instead, he treats the matter seriously and presents through the characters, particularly Dr. Warner, his own suppositions and in some ways romantic and nostalgic feelings about ancient Iran.[28] Similarly, in a story called "S.G.L.L." (1933), which takes place in a futuristic world some two thousand years hence, where human "thirst, hunger, sex, and other needs" have been eliminated and mankind has overcome "aging, disease and ugliness," now only suffering from the incurable ailment of "boredom and alienation," the characters are mostly American, but again Hedayat merely uses them as reflections of his own philosophical concerns.[29]

In several other stories, including "Havasbaz" (1930) [written and published as "Lunatique" in French], "Ayeneh-ye Shekasteh" (1932) [translated into English as "The Broken Mirror"], and "Katya" (1942), again Hedayat chooses Western characters as a vehicle to delineate aspects of his own persona, aspects that are also apparent in his most famous work, *Buf-e Kur* [translated into English as *The Blind Owl*].[30] Suicide, for instance, seems to be a preoccupation with Hedayat, a solution which he employs for Odette, the main character in "The Broken Mirror."[31]

Undoubtedly, one of Hedayat's most sympathetic Western characters is found in "Sag-e Velgard" [The Stray Dog] (1942), the story of a Scottish terrier named Pat, who has lost his loving owner and is left unprotected in the midst of a small town, where he is mistreated by children and adults alike, who consider dogs unclean in accordance with their Islamic beliefs.[32] The story is told from the perspective of the dog, whose eyes, the reader is told, reveal something human about him. And, indeed, Hedayat ascribes many human attributes, thoughts, and emotions to this character. Having been accustomed to a comfortable life with his owner and his family, whom he lost two years earlier, Pat cannot understand why no one gives him any food; instead, he is beaten and driven away by everyone, as if all hold a personal grudge against him. Hedayat sets up a contrast between the life Pat previously lived and his present condition:

> From the time he had fallen into this distant hell two
> winters had passed during which he had not eaten a
> single bellyful of food nor known a peaceful sleep.
> His passions and emotions had been stifled. During
> this time he had not come across a single person who
> would stroke his head or look into his eyes.
> Although people might appear similar to his master,
> nevertheless there seemed to be a world of difference
> between their disposition and behavior and his
> master's. It was as though the people whom he had
> been with before had been closer to his world, had
> understood better his pains and feelings, and had
> protected him.[33]

The fate of this Scottish terrier is inevitably lamentable. The story ends with the terrier overcome with exhaustion after chasing a car in the hope of having found a new owner, lying down in a gutter, knowing full well that he will never be able to get on his feet again. A few hours later, three crows hover above him awaiting his death, ready to pluck out his eyes.

Some critics have viewed "The Stray Dog" as analogous to the conditions in Iran and the life of the common people.[34] Nevertheless, choosing a Western dog as the main character, a dog whose owner is intimated in the story as being a Westerner and who is accustomed to a better life in dramatic contrast to the brutal fate and the inhumane conditions he suffers in Iran, Hedayat juxtaposes aspects of his own society with those of the West, as had been done by such predecessors as Maragheh'i and

Jamalzadeh.

The purpose of Maragheh'i, Jamalzadeh, Hedayat and other writers who advocate change and social reform in their writing is to a great extent didactic. Their criticism of Iranian society notwithstanding, their intention at times is to educate their Iranian audience in the more idealistic social conditions and ways of the progressive West, as they perceive them. The images thus presented are sometimes intentionally quite positive. One such example is a novel by Mohammad Hejazi called *Sereshk* [*Tears*] (1954), in which Hejazi introduces an idyllic picture of America:

> America is a land of greatness. But of all that wonder, what touches my heart most is the love and kindness of its people of every nationality and race who have gathered and joined together in love and kindness. The capital of that country has thousands of good things, but what enchants me most is how pleasantly lush and green that city is. It is a beautiful garden which lies among vast forests and wide rivers.[35]

In the same passage he continues his praise of America and Americans, in particular his guide in this idyllic paradise, a well-known Orientalist scholar, Richard Ettinghausen:

> Had it not been for the companionship of that learned man who possesses inner enlightenment and learning together, I would not have had an enjoyable time away from home in that pleasant garden and among those kindly people.[36]

Hejazi's prefatory description of America and Americans in his novel paints a rather utopian picture of that society, in some respects that of a wonderful landscape, a panoramic canvas prepared as a backdrop for his romantic tale, whose characters are all Americans. The language, tone, characterization, and manipulation of the plot in *Tears* is similar to those of other works by this author, whose stories gained popularity with young, upper-middle-class Iranian readers, particularly women, from the late 1920s on.[37]

Tears opens with a scene in a Washington restaurant at which the narrator encounters a young couple. He is struck with the beauty of the woman. Noting his interest, his friend, the Orientalist scholar, introduces him to a book co-authored by the couple, this becoming essentially a frame used by Hejazi to relate their story.

Told primarily from the point of view of the young man, William, the story is about his life, beginning with his childhood, when his physical beauty sets him apart from other children. With a sense of superiority over others, William believes that few girls could be worthy of him. In fact, his pride prevents him from establishing a close relationship with any of them.

When William is in his early teens, his father, an idealistic architect, dies, leaving the family with little to survive on. Oblivious to the consequential hardships and his mother's suffering to keep up their standard of living, William continues his self-indulgent existence. As he perceives that he has a poetic disposition, he searches in his own mind for the perfect woman, one who would embody both great beauty and a sensitive soul. In his active search for the perfect woman, he befriends an extremely beautiful girl, only to discover that she does not possess a poetic spirit; another young woman whom he admires for her understanding and appreciation of art and beauty, unfortunately, lacks the requisite physical beauty. Eventually he meets and marries Lyda, who, William is convinced, is the girl of his dreams; however, she possesses an excessively jealous nature. She watches his every move and longs to possess him completely, refusing to allow him even to leave the house. In the end, Lyda's paranoiac jealousy reaches such an extreme that in order to prevent William from looking at other women, she blinds him in his sleep. A trial ensues, but William refuses to blame his wife, and the couple resolve to spend the remainder of their lives together.

Despite Hejazi's attempt to present his story as an authentic account of American life with real events and characters, even using the name of an actual American Orientalist scholar to give verisimilitude to his story, *Tears* is essentially escapist fiction dealing with characters and events that have only a very superficial resemblance to reality. In this story, America is presented as a land of prosperity where the only sources of unhappiness are the affairs of the heart. It is a land of opportunity, where financial success is achieved simply by choosing to attain it. The picture that Hejazi paints of American society in *Tears* is in many respects reminiscent of that of many American television soap operas, a popular form of entertainment which was introduced to Iranians a decade or two later.[38] Nonetheless, the accuracy of the image or images that Hejazi presents to the Iranian audience in his popular work is superfluous to the discussion at hand. What is pertinent is that these images left lasting impressions on the psyche of a sizeable portion of the Iranian reading public, particularly young Iranians who followed Hejazi's stories religiously in popular magazines. These impressions of America and Americans were by no means meant to be negative, nor were they intended, as one Russian critic suggests, to be a reflection of the morals of American society, "which are governed by eroticism leading man to complete nervous disorder and crime," or the "depraved tastes of the West."[39] Rather, Hejazi, who simply found America and Americans to be a new vehicle through which to write on his favorite theme, inadvertently and perhaps subconsciously reveals his own views about the locale and characters he has chosen to develop, thereby creating a partly utopian and partly fantastic image of the West and Westerners that functions to allow young Iranian readers to escape from the harsh realities of their daily lives in the early 1950s.[40]

In the context of the political climate of Iran in the early 1950s, when anti-American sentiments were brewing, particularly among the young intellectual groups supporting the nationalistic government of Mohammad Mosaddeq, which was overthrown through clandestine U.S. involvement to restore Mohammad Reza Shah to the throne, Hejazi's enamored vision of America and Americans may be anachronistic. After all, the presence of the Allied occupation forces in Iran in the 1940s and the emergence of the United States as a new power replacing British colonialism were not conducive to positive impressions of Americans on the part of Iranians. But, having served in an administrative capacity some years earlier in a newly established agency, "Sazman-e Parvaresh-e Afkar" [Agency for the Nurturing of Minds], which, as one critic puts it, was intended to develop the "collective mind of Persian citizens,"[41] Hejazi, who appears to have regarded development and modernization as synonymous with Westernization, was in fact being true to the beliefs of many Iranians of his own and the previous generation. Intellectually and emotionally, Hejazi belongs to a generation of the early decades of the twentieth century which looked to the West with admiration, as a model. Certain misgivings about the colonialist powers aside, Western ways, Western education, Western knowledge, Western technology and, on the whole,

Western civilization were admired by these intellectual Iranians, and such misgivings dissipated in regard to America, which resisted categorization as a colonialist power.

Given his status as a high-ranking conservative government official, and undoubtedly his own positive attitude toward the West, Hejazi may have been predisposed to see only the positive aspects of the West and Westerners. But at the same time, the fact should be kept in mind that he wrote first and foremost for a specific Iranian audience, and in many ways America and Americans were merely fictional depictions through which he intended to write about Iran and Iranians.

A similar audience may be the target of a poem entitled "Arus-e Abshar-e Niyagara" [The Bride of Niagara Falls], by an important government and literary figure, Ali Asghar Hekmat, in which he describes an America perhaps even more idyllic than Hejazi's:

Come and listen to one of the hidden
    undivulged mysteries of America(n life)
Many have written on (ritual) secrets but no one
    ever bored a pearl like me
If wealth keeps the heart burning, it also keeps
    the lamp of science and industry alight
In America good luck is hard work; in America
    the star of learning is in the zenith of perfection.[42]

Hekmat goes on to say that America in ancient times "was owned by the tribe of Red Indians," and uses these introductory lines to tell of an ancient native American ritual. What might strike the reader of this poem as rather odd is that in his attempt to educate his compatriots (he was an educator, in fact, a minister of education) about the customs of Native Americans and relay a legend about Niagara Falls, he finds an occasion to praise the new America.

In their idealization of America and Americans, Hekmat and Hejazi are not alone. In contrast to the negative image formed in the minds of many Iranians several decades later, and as opposed to the negative sentiments that existed in the previous and the present century toward the British and the Russians in particular, Iranians generally regarded Americans as sincere in their dealings with them and displayed an affection for them that did not exist with regard to other Westerners. Such sentiments were more or less universal and on occasions expressed in popular poems and songs. One such example is a *tasnif*, or popular song, written by Aref-Qazvini, a noted revolutionary poet and musician, during the Constitutional Revolution, upon the dismissal of the American advisor, Morgan Shuster, who had been brought to Iran to reform the government's chaotic financial system.[43] Shuster's dismissal, which occurred in 1911, was the result of Russian threats and ultimatums. Aref's poem, which was reportedly sung on the streets of Tehran, reveals the popularity of this American advisor and the public sentiments about him:

> Fie and shame on the house where the guest finds at
>   the table not the menu but a notice to
>   depart, my friend.
> Lay down thy life, lay down thy life but suffer not
>   thy guest to go, thy guest to go.
> If *Shuster* goes from Iran, Iran goes to rack and ruin,
>   my friend
> To rack and ruin allow not Iran to go, young men,
>   allow not Iran to go.
> O life of the body, O soul of the world, O real
>   treasure, O eternal pleasure, O *Shuster*!
> May God keep thee here, may God keep thee here;
>   may God, may God, may God keep thee
>   here.
> Our cup is full to the brim [and cannot hold another
>   drop]; the thief is out for theft and the
>   brigand for brigandage, my friend.
> Our history will become the laughing stock of the
>   world if we allow *Shuster* to go from Iran,
>   from Iran Shuster to go.
> O life of the body, O soul of the world, O real
>   treasure, O eternal pleasure, O *Shuster*!
> May God keep thee here, may God keep thee here;
>   may God, may God, may God keep thee
>   here.
> Don't go; though all else may go, heart, head and
>   soul. The eyes of the ill-wisher have turned
>   blind (with rage) because of our unity, my
>   friend.
> Thou art *a part* of us, how can we live *apart* from
>   thee, O *Shuster*? Hence this lament of *'Arif*
>   goes right up to Saturn, right up to Saturn it

goes.

O life of the body, O soul of the world, O real
    treasure, O eternal pleasure, *O Shuster*!
May God keep thee here, may God keep thee here;
    may God, may God, may God keep thee
    here.[44]

    Idyllic and idealistic images of the West are in essence based
on the same incomplete, reconstructed, often selective, and
sometimes distorted vision of the West as were the pictures
presented by the early Iranian travelers who so often focused on
the strangeness of the West. But while the dichotomy between
the Self and the Other may have served to reinforce the
otherness of the Westerners in the works of the nineteenth-
century travelers to the West, it seems to have been utilized in
the works of writers such as Hejazi and Hekmat not merely to
instill a sense of wonder in their audience, but to show them a
glimpse of the ideal, that which is worthy of contemplation and
even emulation. Learning from the West to improve the
conditions in Iran is, of course, nothing new; earlier observers of
the West had also suggested the same, implicitly or explicitly.
This process of learning from the West helped to gradually bring
about a better understanding of and familiarity with the West
and in some ways changed the image of the Other. And even
though the ambivalent attitude of Iranian writers continued, their
portrayal of Western characters became less a picture of strange
alien creatures and more one of familiar figures with lives,
concerns, and emotions similar to their own.

    In Mohammad Mas'ud's *Golha'i keh dar Jahannam Miruyad*
[*Flowers that Grow in Hell*] (1943), for instance, the author makes
an effort to present one of the main characters, Jeannette, in a
most sympathetic way, a character whose foreignness is merely
incidental and in whom "otherness" is less strange than the
portrayal of the Self of the Iranian protagonist in the story.[45]

    Flowers that Grow in Hell is an epistolary novel that begins
with a series of letters to the author by a friend in Brussels.
The letters concern a mutual friend, Mr. D, a young Iranian who
has been educated in Europe and has now suddenly decided to
return to Iran, leaving his wife, Jeannette, behind. Mr. D's
purpose in returning to Iran arises from a sense of duty. As an
educated Iranian whose knowledge and expertise, he feels, is
needed, he wants to serve his country. What worries his friends
is that the Iranian officials in Belgium have reported to the

Iranian government that Mr. D is a communist, which in the late
1930s would almost certainly have led him before a firing squad.
But Mr. D is not sent to the firing squad. Instead, contrary to
his expectations, he is neither offered a position by the
government nor given an opportunity to offer the benefit of his
education. After four years of hopeless struggle in the web of
Iranian bureaucracy, he writes his last letter to his wife, which
comprises the main part of the novel. In it, he describes the
conditions of Iran. On Iranian history, he writes:

> Our ancient history mostly consists of two
> distinct chapters which began at the beginning of our
> society and will end with the end of the world—two
> chapters that follow one another like two lovers or
> like night and day. Throughout our long history,
> these two chapters consist of anarchy and
> dictatorship. Dictatorship is followed by anarchy and
> anarchy followed by dictatorship. Our history is
> comprised of nothing but these two chapters and will
> be so, no matter how one describes it, to the day of
> resurrection.[46]

With these observations about Iranian history and society, he
describes Iran as Hell as opposed to Europe, which he describes
as Paradise. His love for and marriage to Jeannette, a denizen
of "Paradise," therefore, he finds to have been a mistake,
because, as he writes to his wife:

> The word Orient was a mysterious term for you and
> all Europeans. Your feminine curiosity, like that of
> the mother of mankind, Eve, provoked you to reach
> for this forbidden tree. Now, as a punishment for
> this action, you have become a denizen of Hell in
> Paradise.[47]

The portrait of Jeannette in *Flowers that Grow in Hell* is that
of a most sincere and devoted wife and companion who
embodies the ideal qualities that the male Iranian characters of
the novel seek in a woman. On her devotion to her husband,
early in the novel we read in a letter to the narrator-author from
an acquaintance of the couple:

> You have no idea how beautiful, modest, and chaste

this woman is and how much she loves her husband.
I am certain that if she does not see her husband
soon, she will either go mad or commit suicide.[48]

This prediction comes true, and soon after receiving the last
letter from Mr. D, Jeannette kills herself. In her suicide letter to
her mother about her husband she writes that she would not
exchange her love for him for "immortal life." She adds: "He
was a flower from Hell, and I was poisoned upon smelling it.
But the rapture induced by this poison was so pleasurable that
departing from it would be more difficult for me than departing
from life itself."[49]

The portrayal of Jeannette and European life in general is
romanticized to a great extent in *Flowers that Grow in Hell*. But
at the same time, in regards to the nature of the European
powers, the picture that Mas'ud provides is somewhat negative.
Such conflicts as those between England and Russia and England
and Germany are seen as quarrels between giants in the course
of which others, including Iran and Iranians, are trampled and
destroyed. This is symbolized in a dream the protagonist has as
a young man about a female servant caught between two men
who take sexual advantage of her. The young protagonist has
developed an infatuation for the maid, Sakineh, and feels
somehow responsible to protect her. At the same time, he has
been visiting an acquaintance of his father, Mr. Jalil, an
intellectual and a political activist who has been explaining to
him the nature of the wars between the powerful European
governments. In his dream, Sakineh symbolizes Iran and other
weaker nations victimized by strong foreign, Western powers:

I saw the poor Sakineh, pale, gaunt, and naked,
caught between two bloodthirsty executioners. One
of them with angry eyes and frightening face had
pierced her abdomen with a dagger and the other
with a completely calm and solemn face was stuffing
a handkerchief tightly in her mouth to prevent her
from shouting and screaming.

In the midst of this horrible nightmare, in the
darkness of this frightening spectacle, I saw the sorrowful
face of my mother, who was standing next to me with
tearful eyes ... and repeating to me:

"Keep quiet; do not say anything; do not say
anything. These are foreigners; these are foreigners;

these are foreigners."[50]

The two "bloodthirsty executioners" the reader has little difficulty identifying as Russia and England, since a few pages earlier, Mr. Jalil has explained to the young protagonist:

> Unfortunately, we are caught between two strong
> neighbors who have political and economic interests
> in our country. And while they are rivals, they
> cooperate with one another to prevent our progress
> and development.
> The czarist Russians violently and the British
> diplomatically promote the causes of our weakness in
> every respect. In every step that we take to reform
> and improve our own condition, they force us several
> steps backwardswith the fist of power and the finger
> of diplomacy.
> The czarist Russians destroy every reformist step
> we take through ultimatums, and the British rob us of
> any hope of progress by destroying our competent,
> well-wishing, and patriotic officials at our own hands
> with bribery, provocation, and the appointment of the
> most wicked individuals as the leaders of our
> government.[51]

Flowers that Grow in Hell suffers from an abundance of stereotypical representations of the West. Beyond the facade of stereotyping, however, Iranian authors, such as Mohammad Mas'ud, who are more familiar with the West than were their predecessors, see positive aspects even in regard to the Western religion of Christianity.[52]   Comparing the emphasis in Iran placed on religious mourning with what he sees as an optimistic attitude in the West toward religion and life in general, Mas'ud's spokesman is once again Mr. Jalil:

> The secret of the superiority of Europe and the
> grandeur of the Christian nations of the world is that
> they consider the day of Jesus' ascension as a holiday
> and celebrate it.
> Martyrdom is not important to them. They are not
> afraid of death, and whenever their lives are imperfect
> and they are victims of oppression, or when they are
> under economic pressure and their honor and dignity are

threatened, or if they feel that freedom and justice is taken away from them, or they become hungry and distraught, they immediately make an effort to either create a full life for themselves or give up an inferior and shameful life.

They prefer life to death, as long as it is really life, without fear and apprehension, without being poisoned by poverty and hunger, without being victims of injustice and oppression. And if one day there is a shortcoming in the sweet qualities of life and the pleasant cup is poisoned, they will by no means agree to drink a drop of it and prefer heroic death to the continuation of such a squalid life.[53]

Like that of the writers discussed at the beginning of this chapter, in these and other sections of *Flowers that Grow in Hell*, Mas'ud's purpose is also didactic. But in passages such as the one above, the West, again, becomes an ideal model worthy of emulation.

On the whole, in the Persian prose literature written prior to World War II, or perhaps to some extent prior to the 1960s and 1970s, when Persian novels and short stories came of age and developed into relatively mature literary genres in Iran, a process is evidenced, a process of discovery and an attempt on the part of Iranian writers to understand the West and in turn educate their readers about the West. To the more sophisticated observer, such portrayals may at times appear overly shallow and superficial. Despite their superficiality, however, what these Iranian writers admire and what they dislike about the Western Other are no different in essence from that of writers with a more profound knowledge and understanding of the West.

4 THE XENOPHOBIC IMPACT

To see the world in terms of black and white, good and evil is a way to define one's actions, one's attitude and behavior and even at times one's very identity and existence. The Self is often defined vis-à-vis the Other. If the Self demands categorization as good, given that good cannot be defined in the absence of evil, evil must at times be invented, should it seem not to exist.

Simplistic though this premise may be, it is the premise upon which Iraj Pezeshkzad builds one of the most memorable and remarkably true-to-life, albeit caricatured, characters in his very popular novel of the early 1970s, *Da'ijan Napel'on* [*My Dear Uncle Napoleon*].[1] Pezeshkzad's use of this character is rather complex in that it evokes comic sympathy for someone with a familiar political obsession, thereby subtly creating a distance between his reader, who may recognize aspects of Uncle Napoleon's attitude in himself or herself, and the character's obsession, his Anglophobia. The story takes place during World War II, spanning, in fact, the years just before and during the Allied occupation of Iran. The setting is Tehran, the characters essentially members of an extended aristocratic family, and the locale a compound of houses and surrounding courtyard gardens in which different offshoots of the family reside. As the eldest member of the clan, Uncle Napoleon is viewed as the head of the family. His autocratic demeanor toward others is partially responsible for a certain degree of awe and even fear mingled with respect that others feel toward him. But there is also some degree of ridicule, which is most often implied, and at times even articulated, in the attitudes of other family members toward Uncle Napoleon, albeit not in his presence. In fact, Napoleon is the nickname given him by the children because of his admiration for his hero, the French emperor Napoleon Bonaparte. He reads, and has made other family members read, every book

he is able to get his hands on about Napoleon, quotes
(sometimes fabricates quotations from) Napoleon, and generally
tries to emulate him in all his words and deeds.

Uncle Napoleon's devotion to, or rather obsession with,
Napoleon is linked directly to his hostility toward the British.
In fact, he seems possessed by fear of the British, whom he
claims to have fought and defeated in his younger days in a
battle or two, about which, and whether true or not, neither the
members of the family nor the reader are very clear. What is
important is that Uncle Napoleon sees the hand of the British
behind every happening and mishap, whether occurring outside
or within the family. He thinks that the British have been
waiting to avenge their defeats at his hand, regularly sending
secret agents to discredit or destroy him. His fear of the British
often causes discord in the family, especially when he accuses
various family members of being British agents or instruments
of such agents. In reality, the reader can never be sure if indeed
he has had any direct encounters with the British or has even
met an Englishman, for that matter. The image of the British
appears to be a vague composite formed in the mind of the
uncle as the result of his readings of accounts of Napoleon's
adversarial relations with the British, and one could even assume
that his preoccupation with Napoleon's stance against the British
is the reason for his identification with the French general.

The fear of this imaginary adversary, the British, is so
intense that Uncle Napoleon accuses various members of the
household—in one instance his devoted servant, Mash Qasem—of
being British spies. Uncle Napoleon, in fact, arms himself with
a rifle and tries to kill the servant. Other family members
mediate, and when they question Mash Qasem about the matter,
he emphasizes that he has never even seen an Englishman in his
life. Nevertheless, he is so consumed by his master's phobia
that he actually believes he has unwittingly become a British spy
and that he has been instructed to kill Uncle Napoleon.[2] In the
context of the novel, of course, Mash Qasem's behavior is not
surprising, because, according to Uncle Napoleon and, by
extension, Mash Qasem, the British are capable of anything, even
making someone a spy unbeknownst to himself.

The popularity of Pezeshkzad's caricature of Uncle Napoleon
(and Mash Qasem) and the "extraordinary success of the novel,"
as stated in the preface to the 1978–1979 edition, is directly
related to the characters being "natural and tangible, both in
terms of how they live their lives and how they think."[3] In fact,

to Iranian readers they represent the embodiments of a relatively prevalent political philosophy often encountered in their society. To this day, one still hears such phrases as "the British did it" and "the British had a hand in it" from older Iranians of the generation of Uncle Napoleon, and occasionally younger ones who blame the Islamic Revolution of 1978–1979, the overthrow of the Pahlavi dynasty, the coming to power of Ayatollah Ruhollah Khomeini, and the subsequent establishment of an Islamic republic as events designed and orchestrated by the British. Such attitudes, of course, may bring a smile to the faces of the readers of Pezeshkzad's novel, but nonetheless they reveal a lingering image in the Iranian psyche.[4]

The roots of the Anglophobia humorously depicted in Pezeshkzad's novel can be traced to Anglo-Iranian relations in the past, particularly during the Qajar dynasty.[5] Throughout the nineteenth and early twentieth centuries, Iran had become an arena for the rivalry of Western powers vying for influence and ascendancy.[6] Hence, for the generation of Uncle Napoleon, regarding the British with suspicion and blaming them for political events in the country may be somewhat justifiable. Of course, in many instances in real life, as in Pezeshkzad's novel, this suspicion becomes a phobia that extends to all aspects of Iranian life, including the daily affairs of ordinary people.

Pezeshkzad, in fact, draws on the anti-British sentiments prevalent in the country for decades. An earlier expression of such sentiments against the British as oppressive colonialists, sentiments which also ignite patriotic feelings and instill determination in Iranians, is Mohammad Hoseyn Roknzadeh-Adamiyyat's 1931 novel called *Daliran-e Tangestani* [*The Braves of Tangestan*].[7] The setting of this novel is southern Iran during World War I, in the city of Bushehr and the nearby Tangestan area. Subsequent to the Anglo-Iranian hostilities concerning Herat, which was under British control in the nineteenth century, the British, who practically ruled Bushehr at the time, find an opportunity to fly the British flag over the government buildings in that city, convinced that the weak Iranian central government will be unable to oppose them. The British action ignites the fire of patriotism in many Iranians in the city, particularly the local tribal chiefs, who organize a small army to fight the occupying forces. Roknzadeh-Adamiyyat's purpose in writing the novel is two-fold: firstly, to praise the unsung heroes of Iran who fought bravely, despite their small numbers, against the invaders, and secondly, and perhaps as importantly, to provide his reader with a historical, albeit fictional, account of the British colonialist plans for Iran. The British characters are presented as ruthless, cunning individuals lacking all compassion for Iranians. In the novel, the cruelty exhibited by and the characterization of the British are extended to other Europeans as well. The sentiments of Ra'is Ali, the most important anti-British hero of Tangestan, reflect those of the author as well as the audience of the novel two decades later:[8]

> In truth, the Europeans are an oppressive and
> despotic people. Except for having made
> advancements in industry and in making instruments
> of slaughter, they are not superior to us. It is
> astonishing that they consider us savages, while their
> own character and behavior are far worse than that of
> African savages. Is not all this uncalled-for
> bloodshed, all this meaningless slaughter, all this
> injustice, aggression, and cruel-heartedness evidence
> of their savagery and bloodthirstiness? What are all
> these tanks, machine guns, armored ships, and poison
> gases for, except to kill human beings, for quenching
> their [Europeans'] greed and lust, and for other
> materialistic uses?[9]

In contrast to Pezeshkzad's humorous treatment of Anglophobia and more in line with Roknzadeh-Adamiyyat's attitude toward the British, and aesthetically a far superior work, is Simin Daneshvar's best-selling novel, *Savushun* (1969) [translated into English as *Savushun: A Novel About Iran*].[10] The locale of the novel is Shiraz during the Allied occupation of the country in World War II. The story revolves around the lives of a prominent Shiraz family and the reactions of its members to the occupational forces which mainly consist of the British. Yusof, the head of the family, is a headstrong opponent of the foreigners in the city. He openly criticizes the British, often at the risk of endangering his own life and embarrassing others, including Zari, his wife. Unlike *My Dear Uncle Napoleon*, in which the British are a ghostly presence, in *Savushun* they are brought to the foreground. Mainly through the eyes of the protagonist, Zari, but also from the perspective of other Iranians in the story, Daneshvar provides us with portraits of Westerners who have more direct dealings with Iranians. One of the first British characters we meet in *Savushun* is Mr. Zinger, a man who has lived in Shiraz for at least seventeen years but still cannot speak proper Persian and whose name changes to Sergeant Zinger when he dons a military uniform as soon as the war begins. Before the war, Mr. Zinger was a Singer sewing machine salesman, who also gave sewing lessons to his customers. As Zari recalls:

> With every sewing machine he sold, this giant
> corpulent man gave ten free sewing lessons.
> Maneuvering his weight behind the sewing machine,
> he would teach young girls the fine points of
> embroidery, eyelets, and double pleats.[11]

Now that Zari sees Mr. Zinger in an officer's uniform "complete with epaulets and insignia," she reflects on how and why he has lived a lie for all those years:

> She thought, What self-control he must have had to
> live with these lies for seventeen years. A fake
> profession, fake clothes, all lies, from head to toe.
> And how skillful an impostor he was at his job.
> With what cunning he made Zari's mother buy a
> sewing machine.[12]

Zinger's character serves here in the opening pages of the novel as a stereotype of the British in the eyes of Zari, whose perceptions of the British Other are based on preconceptions that seem unaffected by the personal contact with and better knowledge of the British she has had all her life, unlike that of many other Iranians. Zari prides herself on knowing the English and their language and culture quite well, since she "had studied at the British school and her late father had been considered the best English teacher in the city."[13] This kind of stereotypical perception is undoubtedly partly intentional and partly subconscious on the part of the author and is based on her own attitude toward the British. Hence, in the eyes of Zari's husband, Yusof, as well, who also has extensive personal experience with the British—he has, for example, spent some years studying and has received his college education in England—the British in the novel appear in stereotypical form. To Yusof, who sees the world in black and white, they are all the agents of the British colonialist government. Yet the conclusions of Zari, who in regard to other matters is portrayed as a woman capable of seeing shades of grey rather than only black and white, are not much different. The reader is led to conclude that, like Zinger, all the British who have been engaged in various activities and services in the city have lived under one pretext or another, awaiting and preparing for the day they would be called upon to perform their duty as agents of their government. With this perspective, Zari even sees a woman physician whom she has known for a long time as such a functionary of British colonialism. She sees the missionary hospital the British have established as having been part of the preparations to attend to British soldiers, particularly since for some time the beds in the hospital had been used "exclusively for the foreign [i.e., Western] officers and soldiers."[14]

The main bone of contention between Yusof and the British command in the city concerns Yusof's refusal to sell his grain harvest to the British to supply their troops, and the existing food shortages in the city make him more steadfast in this decision. Unlike Yusof, who displays no fear of the British, and in fact often openly and publicly expresses his disdain for them, many other prominent Iranians in the city, including Yusof's own brother, Abolqasem Khan, regard the British with a degree of trepidation combined with admiration. Trying to appease his brother and coax him into selling his crop to the British, Abolqasem Khan says:

> Brother. You're being stubborn for no reason. After
> all, they [the British] are our guests. They won't be
> here forever. Even if we don't give it to them
> willingly, they'll take it by force. They're not
> deterred by the locks and seals on your warehouses.
> And besides, they don't want it for free. They'll pay
> cash for it. ... After all, they are in charge.[15]

Later on in the novel, he reiterates the same idea in the context of the likely reaction of the British to a group of young people who are trying to organize a socialist or Marxist movement. He says:

> Do you think England will just stand by with her
> arms folded watching anybody do whatever the hell
> he wants in the south? You'll see that if the British
> aren't able to buy off all of them together, they will
> buy off a few of their big shots and leaders, and then

woe be it to the fate of the gullible but sincere and
blind believers![16]

The image of the British which is imprinted on the mind of
Abolqasem Khan creates in him fear and awe, which is
sometimes mingled with admiration. He admires them for the
way they preplan, and then proceed to do things according to
plan rather than haphazardly. He is quoted as saying about the
Westerners in general: "See, the Europeans do everything
according to maps and calculations, even their hunting."[17]
Abolqasem Khan's attitude toward the British is, for the
most part, self-serving, as he has been trying to gain their
support to become elected to Parliament. He admires the British
for their planning and calculation in any undertaking, as he
strives to emulate them himself. Indirectly, his admiration for
the British may be in part an affirmation of his own seemingly
planned and calculated ways. He justifies his philosophy and
actions to his brother by saying:

> Brother, why don't you pick up your glass [of wine]?
> I swear to God the world isn't worth crying alone in
> the desert for justice, your frustration gnawing away
> at you. A smart man of the world like myself has
> his smuggled whiskey provided for him. You can't
> refuse to take advantage of these Europeans at all.
> Behind your back, they have the time of their lives
> and laugh at you.[18]

The attitudes of the brothers represent disparate reactions toward
two divergent images of Westerners.   Yusof sees them as
intruders, "uninvited" guests,[19] trying to impose their will on
Iranians. He rebels against them and eventually loses his life.
Abolqasem Khan, on the other hand, fears the Westerners but
has acquiesced to the fate that Iranians in general, himself
included, will never be capable of successfully fighting the
British. Hence, in a sense, unable to beat them at the game, he
has determined to join them. In both cases, the image of the
British is negative. It is an awesome image which generates fear
in the hearts of the people and creates of the Westerners a
monster capable of all evil. In fact, there is even a rumor
among the lower classes that the foreign troops have
contaminated the water reserves with their diseases.
The negative image of the British in *Savushun* is developed

not merely through the portrayal of the British during the time when the Allied occupational forces are present in the city but also in scenes and encounters with the British in the past. In several flashbacks, Zari recalls her school days, when in the British girls' school in the city, the headmistress of the school opposed any sort of Islamic practice or behavior on the part of the Iranian students. For instance, not only did she refuse to include any Islamic religion courses in the curriculum, but, in one scene that Zari recalls vividly, she even cruelly forced a young girl, Zari's friend Mehri, to break her fast during the month of Ramazan:

> The headmistress pushed Mehri down to the
> classroom floor, sat by her head, opened her mouth
> with her hands, put a finger in her mouth and tried
> to pour water down her throat. Mehri bit the
> headmistress's hand and the headmistress shouted
> angrily, "You miserable wretch!" Then Mehri sat up
> and said, "The filthy hand of you, an infidel, touched
> my mouth, so my fast is automatically broken. Give
> me the water; I'll drink it all. You'll be responsible
> for the sin."[20]

In another scene, Zari recalls how the headmistress forced her to remove the black blouse she was wearing as a sign of mourning for her recently deceased father and to wear a white one instead, all because some British visitors were coming to the school and Zari was expected to recite a poem by Kipling to welcome them. Zari recounts the incident and proudly recalls that at the opportune moment, when she was to recite Kipling's "If," she defiantly recited Samson's opening speech in Milton's play *Samson Agonistes*: "O dark, dark, dark, amid the blaze of the noon."

Virtually the only exception to the negative representation of Westerners in *Savushun*, one in which the image of a Westerner is treated somewhat sympathetically, is with regard to an Irish poet serving in the city as a war correspondent. MacMahon is an old friend of Yusof and, like Yusof, he is also fighting for his country against the British. For MacMahon, his weapon is his poetry. In a drunken stupor one night, speaking to Yusof, he compares Iran and Ireland and their struggle for independence:

Oh Ireland, oh land of Aryan descendants, I have
composed a poem about a tree that must grow in
your soil. This tree is called the Tree of
Independence. This tree must be irrigated with
blood, not water. Water will dry it up. Yes, Yusof,
you were right. If independence is good for me, it is
good for you too. And that story you told me was
very useful to me. You told me about the tree in
your legends, whose leaves when dried and applied
to the eyes like *kohl*, can make one invisible and
capable of doing anything. I wish there were one of
these trees in Ireland and one in your city.[21]

The obvious parallels that MacMahon draws between Iran and
Ireland reinforce the negative image of the British as the evil
adversary of both. In a sense, MacMahon is a device, a
representative of other oppressed people and nations of the
world, who happens to be a Westerner himself. But even in this
case, his is not an altogether sympathetic image. He is
portrayed as a stereotypical Irishman, always drinking or drunk,
and is even a target of suspicion for Yusof's son Khosrow who,
like his father, believes all the British to be agents of their
government, and therefore suspects MacMahon of being a spy
since he does not wear the uniform of a military officer.

The negative image of the British as portrayed in the novels
discussed appears to be essentially the result of the imperialist
policies of England and the English in Iran. Such attitudes were
perpetuated in the post–World War II era, particularly during the
period of Mosaddeq and the oil nationalization movement when,
for Mosaddeq and the nation as a whole, the target of negative
sentiments was primarily the British. It is also helpful to
remember that both Iraj Pezeshkzad and Simin Daneshvar, for
instance, like many other prominent writers of the decades of the
1960s and 1970s, had been witness to this period in Iranian
history; therefore, the images they provide in their respective
novels are inevitably influenced by their experiences of the
Mosaddeq era.

"The fall of Mosaddeq," confesses Daneshvar in an interview
after the Islamic Revolution, "was a very harsh slap in the face
by history that we [the intelligentsia] and the oppressed Iranian
nation suffered together."[22] The images of the British in
particular, who were Mosaddeq's adversary in the oil
nationalization movement, in these stories are created in response

to the British role in his overthrow. For Daneshvar's generation, the traumatic impact of this event lingers on. Literary artists writing two or three decades later have been unable to forgive and forget the British role in the overthrow of Mosaddeq. The British often appear as an abstraction of evil forces behind the scene that manipulate and control Iran and Iranians. The writer often expresses frustration and retaliates by presenting the British as the arch-villain in his or her work. The negative image of the British is often combined with that of the Iranian government in works of anti-establishment writers. An example is Ahmad Mahmud's *Hamsayehha* [The Neighbors], published in 1974.[23]

Mahmud's novel is the story of Khaled, a young man from a working-class family, and his exposure to and involvement in dissident anti-government political activities. The story begins during the Mosaddeq era. The locale is the oil-rich province of Khuzestan, and hence the issue of oil nationalization and the British involvement in it are tangible to the characters of the novel. Mahmud recreates the general social and political climate of this period in his story. Anti-British sentiments are widespread in the society, and political discussions and demonstrations are commonplace in the streets. The British are referred to as "bloodthirsty colonialists" and the "beast who only drinks blood and whose appetite is never satisfied."[24] Khaled is still too young to readily understand the meaning of these phrases that he hears on the streets or reads with difficulty in political handouts. Blood, he eventually learns, stands for oil, for which the British have an unquenchable thirst. He understands that everyone wants the British to leave, but he is confused by the contradictory statements he hears about them. A worker with a ribbon pinned to his chest on which the words are written, "The oil industry must be nationalized," argues about a "lion" with another worker. "So you have also stuck one of these ribbons on your chest?" remarks one worker to the other rhetorically, adding, "You cannot pull the lion's tail with such statements." The man with the ribbon on his chest responds, "The lion has gotten old, friend. ... He has lost his hair," and then continues his political speech: "That time is over; the period of plunder has ended. The lion must now put its tail between its legs and get lost. Now everything has an owner; everything must be accounted for."[25]

Khaled begins to understand that the "lion" is a reference to the British and wonders, "What are the British doing in our country anyway?" and, "What does our oil have to do with the

British?"[26]   But Khaled also hears the prime minister on the radio warning against driving the British out of the country:

> If we nationalize the oil industry, we will be
> destroyed. To throw the British out is a mistake. ...
> We have no petroleum engineers; yet our economy is
> based solely on oil. If they become obstinate and
> refuse to purchase our oil, we will go bankrupt.[27]

The prime minister, however, is immediately accused of being a "British functionary," a man about whom it is said, "As long as he is in power, the British have nothing to fear."[28]

In the midst of this confusion, Khaled's early education in politics is completed. In the later years of his life, when he becomes an active political dissident, for which he is interrogated, tortured, and jailed, he carries with him the implied understanding that his fight against the government and the British is in essence one and the same. And Khaled's creator, Ahmad Mahmud, like Simin Daneshvar, seeks symbolic revenge for the eventual failure of the Mosaddeq government, which attempted to "throw the British out." He recreates a scene in the novel in which an effigy of an Englishman is burned by the populace in celebration of the oil nationalization:

> In the city square, people made an effigy of an
> Englishman with cloth, rags, and sticks and wanted to
> set it on fire. They had put a pair of short trousers
> on the effigy and had soiled its crotch with black oil.
> They had placed a wide-rimmed hat on its head.
> From the butcher's shop, they had taken the penis of
> a bull and stuffed it between the effigy's lips in place
> of a cigar. And the effigy had a little dog, which
> was dragged after him on a chain. It was made of
> cloth and rags. It had large floppy ears and was
> colored with black oil. People were crowding around
> the effigy of the Englishman and cheering.[29]

Such negative images regarding the British linger even in stories published in the 1980s. In his "Ruz-e Nahs" [The Sinister Day], another story about the Mosaddeq period, Asghar Elahi recounts the sentiments of many Iranians toward the British and their wish to "throw the British out."[30]   The images are reminiscent of Mahmud's novel. The narrator is a child looking out the window at the street, describing the people crowding around a baboon that has been given a cane and a hat to make him look like Winston Churchill. A middle-aged spectator beats the monkey and the crowd cheers him on.[31]

With the crushing of the Mosaddeq movement, the negative sentiments began to shift from the British to the Americans. The diminishing British power meant to many Iranian writers that British colonialism was being replaced by American neocolonialism. Simin Daneshvar, for instance, in the interview cited above in this chapter, refers to the United States as the originator of this new kind of colonialism. The military coup d'etat led by General Zahedi and his supporters to reinstate the shah became widely recognized as having been orchestrated and financed by the CIA.[32] Also, American influence in Iran began to increase, and within a period of a few years, Americans gained not only more influence in Iran but, with this influence inherited from the British, gained also the legacy of the negative image of the British. Negative images of Americans began to appear increasingly in Persian literature during these two decades, notably in the works of such writers as Jalal Al-e Ahmad (1923–1969).

A well-known writer of the 1960s, Al-e Ahmad composed short stories, novels, ethnographic studies, travel diaries, and polemical essays focusing on socio-political themes. Unlike in the works of Iraj Pezeshkzad, Simin Daneshvar, and Ahmad Mahmud, in Al-e Ahmad's writings the authorial voice resonates, often loudly and clearly, throughout both his nonfictional work, in which his style is direct without any attempt to hide behind a dispassionate scholarly mask, and his fiction, in which he tries to disguise this authorial voice behind that of a narrator.

Al-e Ahmad's most influential polemical work is *Gharbzadegi* (1962) [translated into English as *Plagued by the West* and *Weststruckness*], an essay of some two hundred pages which, despite being banned during the Pahlavi era, was widely circulated and read in Iran.[33] The popularity of *Plagued by the West* may have been due to its successful voicing of the sentiments of many Iranians concerning Western influences in Iran, particularly in response to the government's efforts to modernize the country.

In *Plagued by the West*, Al-e Ahmad divides the world into two poles, the developed industrial countries, which he calls the West, and the underdeveloped countries, which he calls the East. "For me," he writes, "'West' and 'East' have neither political nor geographic meaning. Instead they are two economic concepts. 'West' means the well-fed countries and 'East' means the hungry countries."[34] He characterizes the West as comprised of countries with "high wages, low mortality rates, low birth rates, well-organized social services, adequate nutrition," even specifying the number of calories, at least 3,000 per day, a "per capita income of more than 3,000 tomans ($430) per year, and a democratic facade inherited from the French revolution," as opposed to Eastern countries with reverse characteristics.[35] Then, stating that obviously "we belong to this second group,"[36] he expounds the dichotomy of the West and the East as follows:

> One pole belongs to the well-fed, the rich, the
> powerful, the producers and exporters of
> manufactured products; whereas the other pole is that
> of the hungry, the poor, the weak, and the consumers
> and importers. The pulse of progress beats on that
> side of the world of ascendance and the throb of
> decline on this side of a world petering out. The
> difference does not merely arise out of temporal or
> spatial dimensions, nor is it measurable in terms of
> quantity—it is a qualitative difference. The two poles
> are estranged from one another. They are inclined
> towards mutual remoteness. On that side is a world
> which is frightened of its own dynamism and on this
> side is our world which has not yet been able to find
> a way to channel its undirected and therefore wasted
> energies. Both of these worlds are in motion, each in
> a different direction.[37]

It is this image of the West and Westerners that appears in Al-e Ahmad's fiction as well, often indirectly, but occasionally directly. Unlike Simin Daneshvar in *Savushun*, which was published in 1969 but deals with the World War II period and whose antagonists are the British, as an outspoken post–World War II writer who dealt generally and directly with topical social issues,[38] Al-e Ahmad focuses on contemporary issues and chooses American characters in his portrayal of Westerners. In his most popular novel, *Modir-e Madreseh* (1958) [translated into English as *The School Principal*], which deals essentially with the ills of the educational system in Iran, the only foreign character in the book, an American who is introduced to the reader indirectly and is in fact a stereotype, functions not unlike the

British in Iraj Pezeshkzad's *My Dear Uncle Napoleon*.[39]   The
protagonist-narrator of the story, with whom and whose plight
many Iranian readers of Al-e Ahmad of the time identified, is a
character resembling the author himself. Disenchanted with the
educational and indeed with the entire political and bureaucratic
system in the country, the narrator had hoped to disengage
himself from involvement in the system by accepting a position
in an isolated area, a position he thinks will allow him to do so.
In practice, however, his experiences prove to be to the contrary,
as he faces the chaotic effects and problems that the system has
created even in a small rural community outside Tehran, where
he has now become the new school principal. One day he is
informed that one of his teachers has been hit by a car belonging
to one of the Americans who had recently moved into town "in
order to bring water and electricity along with him to the
area."[40]   The American is actually never mentioned by name,
nor do we know anything else about him. But a few pages
later, when visiting the injured teacher in the hospital, the
principal questions rhetorically:

> Why, why? Why did you have to flaunt that great
> Director General's body everywhere you went until
> they finally got you, until they ran you down? You
> mean to say you didn't know that a teacher has no
> right to cut such a figure? Why did you have to be
> such an eye-stopper? You used to be even too big
> for the foot paths. You used to block the
> thoroughfare. Didn't you know that streets and
> traffic lights and civilization and pavement all belong
> to those who, in cars built in their own country,
> trample the rest of the world?[41]

The ambiguity of the third person plural pronoun in this
passage is, of course, intentional. To the reader it vacillates
between references to the Iranian government and the Americans.
At the same time, it allows Al-e Ahmad to escape the wrath of
the censors, who would not have tolerated any criticism of the
Pahlavi regime. But it also succeeds in articulating the idea that
the shah's government and the United States are one and the
same, since the shah is a functionary of the Americans. As for
the last part of these reflections, they are indeed a dramatization
of Al-e Ahmad's characterization of the West and Westerners set
forth in his *Plagued by the West*.

A similar but somewhat more direct portrayal of the West and Westerners also appears in a short story entitled "Showhar-e Amrika'i" (1969) [translated into English as "The American Husband"].[42]   The story is presented as the monologue of an Iranian woman who has recently divorced her American husband. She finds out that although she was led to believe that her husband is a "lawyer," he turns out to be a grave digger. This "tragedy of error" is, according to the story, based on the young woman's misinterpretation of the term "layer" for "lawyer." The Iranian reader unfamiliar with English must take for granted that the word for "undertaker" or "mortician" is "layer." What is significant, as it relates to the general image of Americans presented in the work, is that Al-e Ahmad writes this story because he has an axe to grind, so to speak, against Americans.   For this reason, he manipulates the English lexicon—regardless of whether or not he is actually conscious of his misuse of the language—to arrive at the image he intends to present.   In any case, the Iranian woman and most of the members of her family are enamored of the young American and pleased when he asks her to marry him. At that time, he is a teacher of English in a language institute where she attends classes. After their marriage, the couple move from Tehran to Washington, where eventually, through his former fiance, the wife finds out about her husband's actual occupation, which she considers appalling, but with which the Americans on the whole see nothing wrong.

Even though Al-e Ahmad uses the ploy of telling the story entirely from the point of view of the Iranian woman, the story presents the same perception concerning America and Americans which is based on a polarized view of the world, as discussed earlier in his *Plagued by the West*, and all the characters are based on stereotypes. For example, speaking of an American woman who is married to an Iranian, now a member of the Iranian Parliament, the narrator explains:

> The girl spoke with a Texas drawl—no, don't laugh;
> I'm not kidding—and she would open her mouth so
> wide. It was obvious that she used to wash large
> stacks of dishes every day. And then do you know
> what she said? She said, "We have come here and
> brought you civilization and taught you how to use a
> gas stove and a washing machine ..." and things like
> that. From her hands you could tell that in Texas

she still washed clothes by hand in a tub. And they
put on such airs! She was the daughter of a
cowboy—not the kind on whose land oil is discovered
and they get to be too big for their britches. No, she
was one of those who tended somebody else's
cattle.[43]

The narrator's reaction to the claim of the American woman
is that of the writer himself and displays his attitude toward
Western civilization in general and what it offers to non-
Westerners. Al-e Ahmad's further response to such claims is put
in the mouth of yet another character in the story: "If
civilization consists of the things you are talking about, the same
company that sends you along with the washing machine as a
present to us can keep it."[44] This is in fact the attitude that
persists throughout the story. The American husband's former
fiance has been engaged to two other men before. One was
killed in the Korean war, another in Vietnam. The third one, the
husband of the Iranian woman, who was also in Korea, came
back a changed man. "God knows what they did to the young
people in Korea that when they returned they would accept such
professions," the former girlfriend tells the wife, continuing that,
"in fact, it's hard to figure out why those of them who come
back either take such odd jobs or turn into madmen, thieves, and
murderers."[45]

Al-e Ahmad's negative portrayal of America and Americans
in this story is represented in his detailed description of the
husband's profession and also the presentation of the capitalist
system through its funeral industry. Visiting the "office" where
the husband is employed, the wife comments on how the people
in the funeral home, thinking of her as a prospective customer,
try their sales pitch on her:

Such attractive pictures of parks, trees, and lawns. If
you did not know what the place was for, you would
think they were building homes for honeymooners.
And everything with charts and maps, all with
dimensions, sizes, hinges, and handles on both sides,
and flowers on the top. And what kind of wood
would you prefer? And what kind of cloth would
you like to cover it with? And what kind of service?
And the hearse that takes you away, how many
horses should it have? Or, if you wish, we can use

an automobile, which is cheaper. Such a mechanized
system! How many people you want in the
procession and what their wages would be, and how
much emotion they should display, and each of them
will play the role of a relative, and how they will
dress, and what church.[46]

His partly accurate and partly imagined or fabricated description
of the American funeral industry presents America as a society
in which even death is utilized to sell capitalist commodities,
and everything, including emotions, has a price. In one sense,
the Iranian wife feels she has been deceived and exploited by
the American husband, who even while in Iran, the wife realizes
now, was trying to start a funeral industry with another
American, an advisor to the Iranian Plan and Budget
Organization, since it would require very little in the way of
capital investment.[47] Here, Al-e Ahmad may indirectly be using
this marriage as a metaphor for the relations between the United
States and Iran. The American husband's profession in the
funeral industry, a term which Al-e Ahmad uses synonymously
with grave digger in this story, is further used to signify the
role America plays with regard to the rest of the world. In
other words, America is the grave digger of the world. An
Iranian friend of the wife in Washington, who hears of her
dilemma, observes that Americans "are all of this profession;
they do it for the whole human race."[48]

The West as the exploiter of the East is a recurrent theme
in much of Al-e Ahmad's work. Although not as directly as in
Plagued by the West or "The American Husband," he had already
treated this theme in an earlier story, *Sargozasht-e Kanduha* [*The
Story of the Beehives*], published in 1955.[49] In this story, Al-e
Ahmad employs the format of a fable about a farmer, Kamand
Ali Beyg, who has by chance learned the art of beekeeping. He
keeps twelve hives, which provide him a substantial income
without having to labor from sunrise to sunset, as do the other
farmers in his village. For this reason, he has become the envy
of the entire village. The bees do the work and Kamand Ali
Beyg simply reaps the benefit. The story, however, focuses on
the exploited bees, who have come to realize that all their hard
work storing food for the winter comes to naught, as every year
"calamity" strikes, their food is taken away, and many of them
become victims of the mishap. Even though their stored honey
is replaced with date syrup, the wiser members of the bee

colony are aware that the continuation of the situation would mean their annihilation. Hence, eventually, the elder bees decide that they must free the colony from the exploiter, and one morning they all leave Kamand Ali Beyg's hives for their ancestral home in the mountains where there is an abundance of flowers and a river.

Critics have observed that *The Story of the Beehives* is Al-e Ahmad's attempt at writing a parable on the failure of Dr. Mosaddeq's National Front movement and how the Western companies gained the upper hand in the oil nationalization conflict. In other words, Kamand Ali Beyg represents the Western powers, who had succeeded in contriving their exploitation of the Iranians. As one critic points out, however, the parable fails in that the "active and orderly life of the honeybees does not reflect life in an Iran plagued by the colonialism" of those years.[50] Moreover, it is uncertain how we are to interpret the departure of the bees, not to mention the uncertainty of their destination. Nevertheless, the mysterious outsider, Kamand Ali Beyg, apparently represented the West to Al-e Ahmad and his audience at the time and reinforced the image of the Westerners as subjugators and economic exploiters.

Readers are wont to interpret the story as a condemnation of Western exploitation despite the fact that *The Story of the Beehives* contains no direct reference to any particular Westerners, and Al-e Ahmad does not identify the exploiter as a representative of the West or Western powers, as he does in *The School Principal*, "The American Husband," and *Plagued by the West*. The latter work, of course, has had a lingering effect on the following generations of fiction writers, in whose works Americans appear as the Western exploiter.

The image of the American as the exploiter appears in a short story, "Dandil" [translated into English as "Dandil"], by Gholamhoseyn Sa'edi (1935–1985), a prominent fiction writer and playwright of the 1960s, 1970s, and 1980s.[51] The persona that Sa'edi chooses to represent the exploiter is a military officer. Dandil is the name of the infamous red-light district in Maragheh, a small town in northwestern Iran. The story revolves around a fifteen-year-old virgin who has recently been brought to one of the houses and for whom the pimps are trying to find a munificent first customer. Upon the advice and with the help of the neighborhood policeman, they succeed in finding an American sergeant who is expected to bring prosperity to this poverty-stricken, disease-infested neighborhood. In his attempt to sell the idea of having the American as the first customer, the policeman presents an image of America and Americans which, in contrast to Dandil and its people, is that of a modern fairyland filled with prosperous people:

> I'm talking about that dude. They're not poor and starving like us. I swear to God, they're always rolling in cash.
> Wherever they go, they spend money like crazy. They pay up and they want to have a good time. But I'm telling you, when he comes here, everything's got to be the way he likes it, because he's going to pay for it all. Just think of it—the dude's a sergeant, but his pay is three times more than our boss gets. Just go to the army base and see the way he's living. It'll surprise the hell out of you. Even the big shots stand at attention for him. So, with a man like that coming here, do you realize how much Dandil is going to improve? You'll have it made, but not the way things are now, with all this filth. Can we bring him in the dark? They're not used to this kind of mess. In their country, the days and nights are the same. In fact, their nights are even brighter than their days.
> I've seen pictures of their cities. The buildings are all glass, and the streets sparkle like crystal. There's rows and rows of banks, and every one of 'em is full of money. They're not beggars like us. They all have private cars. Their whores spend four or five hours a day just playing around in the beauty shops.[52]

Finally, the neighborhood is cleaned up, lights are placed in various corners and food and drink prepared for the evening when the guest will come to call.

Sa'edi's characterization of the American sergeant sharply contrasts with the policeman's earlier picture of the "civilized" Westerner. He is described as:

> a huge, fat American who was stumbling as he walked. ... He had a big head with little hair and beady eyes. He had a triple chin. He was wearing an open-necked shirt and tight Bermuda shorts. He

had flung his thin jacket over his shoulder, and he
seemed to be punching the air with his fist. A
cigarette was hanging from his lips. He ignored
everybody.[53]

In fact, the American is portrayed as a savage of sorts, only
capable of clownish gestures and nonsensical utterances. Seeing
the crowd of onlookers who have gathered to watch him, he
roars and charges the crowd.   With the people frightened
somewhat, as if by a strange beast, the narrative continues:

The Sergeant fell to his knees in laughter; slapping
his thighs, he yelled and howled, "Yo-ho-ho-ho ... Yo-
ho-ho-ho!" The crowd huddled in the shadows and
booed him.[54]

The next morning, having spent the night with the new prize
prostitute, the American leaves without paying. No money had
been collected from him in advance lest he be offended. It is
again the police officer who sums up the situation. This time
the picture he gives of the American is neither that of
respectable rich man, nor of a clownish beast, but a destructive
monster:

You can't say nothing to him. You can't go asking
him for bread. He's not like you and me; he's
American. If he gets pissed off, if he's not satisfied,
he's going to turn Dandil inside out. He'll kill us all
and destroy everything.[55]

The climate in which Sa'edi as well as other writers, some
of whom have been discussed briefly in this chapter, wrote was
one in which Western influence, both politically and culturally,
seemed to many Iranians uncontrollable. The works of writers
such as Iraj Pezeshkzad, Simin Daneshvar and Ahmad Mahmud
chronicle the reactions of Iranians to these influences, which
were regarded as a threat to the political, and perhaps more
importantly the cultural, foundations of their society. The works
of other writers, such as Jalal Al-e Ahmad and Gholamhoseyn
Sa'edi, on the other hand, display more direct signs of this
xenophobic impact and indeed become themselves the literary
representations of dissent against the Western influences in Iran.
Nevertheless, it should be kept in mind that anti-Western

sentiments of the kind discussed here do not stem from a sense of hatred for the Other, in this case, the West. Rather, they should be viewed as Iranian reactions to the Western cultural and political threat, the purpose of which is ultimately self-protection and the preservation of their cultural and political identity.

5

SPLIT IMAGES

In the novels and short stories examined in the previous chapter, the images presented of the British and Americans are generally negative and characteristically stereotypical. Such negative images in the minds of Iranians as depicted by novelists and short story writers perhaps reflect what Iranian writers saw as the attempts by Westerners to exploit Iranians and their country for economic gain and political control. These reactions took the form of fear and helplessness vis-à-vis the awesome and powerful image of the West created in the Iranian psyche as well as resentment and rejection of the West as a corrupting influence that undermined the authentic Iranian values and identity. Whatever the form of the reactions, they were based, consciously or subconsciously, on a dichotomy of the Self and the Other, black and white, good and evil.

Despite the complexity of the causes and roots of such attitudes, the reactions themselves are simple and unambiguous, precisely because the function of such negative images is primarily self-defense. But the creation of negative images of the West, in the form of stereotypical characters, for instance, is also an attempt to place the blame for all the societal ills of Iran on the adversary, as exemplified by many of the stories already discussed, such as Pezeshkzad's *My Dear Uncle Napoleon*, Simin Daneshvar's *Savushun*, and Jalal Al-e Ahmad's *The School Principal* and "The American Husband."

Iranian attitudes toward the West, however, are not always as clearly delineated and defined as in the case of the stories mentioned above. Much of Persian fiction treats the dilemma of the encounter with the West with ambivalence. When faced with the reality and the inevitability of Western influence, many Iranian writers take a more introspective look at their society and hesitate to place on the West complete blame for the problems and inadequacies in it. Thus, the images of the West and Westerners are not always depicted as totally negative and evil, and the Iranian literary artist makes use of other shades and colors in presenting such images. This ambivalent attitude can be found not only in the travel diaries and fiction of the nineteenth and early twentieth centuries, but also continues in works written after World War II. One such work is Hoseyn Madani's popular adventure story, *Esmal dar Niyuyork* [*Esmal in New York*], which was first serialized in *Sepid va Siyah* [Black and White] magazine and soon after published in book form in the early 1950s.[1]

Esmal in New York can in one respect be read as a fictional travel diary following the tradition of the nineteenth-century writings in that genre. In keeping with those works, an Iranian traveler sets out on a journey to the West, with descriptions of the places and people he sees that are reminiscent of earlier Iranian travelers' visits to "Wonderland."

Unlike the writer-narrators of the travel diaries, who were usually well-educated men of means, the protagonist of Madani's novel is an uneducated truck driver, whom the author describes as a "*jahel*," a member of the brotherhood of streetwise roughnecks found in many Iranian cities.[2] The story takes place during World War II, when the Allied forces occupied Iran. Esmal has befriended William, an American soldier, from whom he learns that in the United States a driver such as he can make eight dollars, or fifty tomans, compared to the fifteen tomans a day he makes in Iran. Hence, Esmal decides to visit the United States. With the help of his American friend, Esmal finds a job on the ship that is taking William back home.

Madani spices his story with a great deal of humor, partly through the use of slang expressions that are a part of the language of "*jahel*"-type characters such as Esmal and partly by placing him in situations which illustrate the sharp disparities in the two cultures. At the same time, the images of the West and Westerners that are presented are not always from the perspective of Esmal, but also of the author himself. In fact, on many occasions, the narrator-author directly addresses the reader with commentary about Western customs, ideas, and beliefs, and, on the whole, the Western character. Observations and generalizations about Western women, Western conscience, and Western morality are presented unabashedly throughout the book, at times expressed through the protagonist and often directly by the narrator. On the other hand, the story of Esmal's encounter with America and Americans gives the author an opportunity to show his readers the positive sides of the alien culture and its technological advancements. Madani's novel is in some respects like a double-edged sword. By juxtaposing the two cultures, his criticism is directed toward both.

One of Esmal's first encounters with Western morality and Western women is with Catherine, a maid in the Waldorf Astoria Hotel in New York, where Esmal and William are staying.[3] Fascinated by the beautiful Catherine, a woman in her late twenties, Esmal asks her why she is not married. Catherine answers that she has just recently divorced her husband and that she does not want to be married again, because she will not be able to find a man who would embody all the good qualities of each of her previous four husbands in terms of wealth, talent, and good looks. Esmal assumes Catherine to be a typical American woman, whom he compares with Iranian women, his only frame of reference. The only Iranian women he knows who could match Catherine in the number of men with whom they have been intimate are prostitutes. Hence, he observes sarcastically, "How chaste you foreign women are, really! When one sees things like this, one appreciates one's own homeland. How wonderful are the chaste women of Tehran ... who only marry one husband in their whole life, ... not like you."[4] Such scenes occur frequently in Madani's novel, in which the unconstrained attitudes of American women are criticized and contrasted with those of Iranian women.

A scene in which Esmal is traveling on the subway in New York City clearly reveals such an attitude:

At this time, a young, beautiful girl approached where they [Esmal and a woman friend] were sitting, and since there were no seats available, she stood in the aisle. A handsome young man with a cigarette in his mouth was sitting across from Esmal. When the young man saw the girl, he offered to let her sit on his lap. (In New York, such behavior is not considered improper, and there is absolute freedom.)[5]

Even without the interjection of the author in the form of his parenthetical remark, the continuation of the scene and the absence of any reaction by other passengers reveal the narrator's and Esmal's judgment about American morality and women. But the scene continues even further, with the young man starting to

fondle the woman's breast, which action eventually outrages
Esmal and results in a fight between him and the young man.[6]
However, in the end, when the police intervene, Esmal is blamed
for the fight, issued a five-dollar fine, and told that he has
behaved like an animal.

Madani's criticism of the Americans and American society
also extends to the condition of black Americans who live in
poverty.   After Esmal's visit to Harlem, which takes place
despite the reluctance of his friend, William, the reader is
told:

> Esmal was upset because of the living conditions of the
> black people and blamed their misfortune and
> destitution on the great leaders. He knew well that
> the results of the round-the-clock labor of these
> unfortunate people and thousands like them scattered
> around the world in every country who live under
> similar conditions furnishes the comfort of the leaders
> in their eiderdown beds.[7]

In this case, it is not the protagonist but in fact the author who
makes these observations, with respect to which Madani is in
conformity with many of his contemporary intellectuals and
writers in Iran.   In fact, the author overlooks few opportunities
to blame the leaders of the Western world for the ills that exist
in the world and for their condescending attitude toward Iran.
The West, according to Madani and his protagonist, has made
advancements in technology, for instance, and regards itself
civilized, but it is also responsible for global wars and the
creation of weapons of destruction.   Glancing at an American
newspaper, Esmal sees pictures of military commanders in the
ongoing war in Europe, of battle scenes, of slaughtered soldiers
and then of Western leaders—Churchill, Roosevelt and Stalin:

> The more he looked, the sadder his face would
> become. For a while, he would look at the picture of
> soldiers who were killed, at the photograph of bomb
> explosions and then for a moment at the pictures of
> the leaders of the three governments.[8]

Madani once again finds an occasion for pontification about the
West from the perspective of an Iranian like Esmal:

Even though he had grown up in a backward country
and even though he was reared in a country that
according to foreigners [i.e., Westerners] is lacking in
culture and education, he cursed from the bottom of
his heart the civilized and cultured warmongers. Even
though he had yet to understand the meaning of the
concepts of politics, civilization, and freedom, he knew
full well that freedom and civilization would endure in
a country only when the people and nations learn to
live in true peace and tranquility.[9]

But at the same time, Esmal's visit to the United States is a
vehicle through which Madani shows the wonders and
advancements of the West and indirectly criticizes the Iranians
in an attempt to make them aware of their backwardness. To do
so, on many occasions, for example, he places his protagonist in
situations in which Esmal finds the laws and regulations
dictating social behavior too confining, and he wishes he could
be back in Iran where he is free to do anything he wants. An
incident that illustrates the rule of law and social behavior in the
West, and which Madani uses to humorously point to the
contrast in the attitude of Iranians toward law and order, occurs
on a train. Madani's description of the American railroad
system and the comforts it provides for passengers, including
restaurants, bars, dancing and card playing rooms, as well as
attendants and even the music and news piped into all
compartments, presents to the Iranian reader an enviable picture
of an America which is progressive, prosperous, and orderly.
The author's commentary on how happily Americans live also
contributes to this picture:

Americans always want to spend their time in
entertainment, gaiety, and having a good time. They
dance in cafes, play guitars and saxophones in the
streets, and even sing in the restrooms and bathrooms.
And because the government officials are aware of
what people are like, when ordering railroad cars, they
also order one for singing and dancing. On the whole,
it must be pointed out that the Americans are happy
and have a good time, whether they are working or
not, whether they are on a trip or at home.[10]

In the midst of this picture, Madani then places his uneducated,

Iranian protagonist, who is ignorant of the codes of behavior in such an alien environment. At one point, Esmal decides that he would like to take some fresh air. He simply climbs on the roof of the train to sit and even invites his embarrassed friend William to join him. Once the train officials learn of the situation and sound the whistle to warn him of the danger and ask him to come back into the car, Esmal stands up and begins to run and jump from the roof of one car to the next. The train is stopped and Esmal comes down, but he is put under arrest. To free him from detention, William speaks to the chief conductor of the train. His words are, in fact, Madani's addressed indirectly to his Iranian readers:

> Chief, I am very sorry for my friend, who disobeyed
> the rules causing you to place him in detention. But I
> must explain that he is an Iranian, and Iranians, as you
> know, are from a very backward society. You have
> not visited their country—I have just been there and I
> have seen so many things with my own eyes—if you
> had, you would think these people had escaped from
> the heart of Africa and gone there. I swear to you
> that, besides the fact that they have no inkling of
> civilization, most of their actions resemble those of
> savages. I beg of you to release him, because "to
> Iranians, prison and liberty are one and the same!"
> [Emphasis in the original.][11]

William's observation about Iranians being unable to distinguish between prison and liberty is obviously Madani's implicit commentary on the Iranian political system. The Iranian reader is presumed to recognize that he lives in a large prison called Iran and does not, therefore, understand the meaning of freedom, as does the Westerner.

On the whole, the author of *Esmal in New York* approaches the West with a mixed, even equivocal attitude. Esmal's final observations about the United States for his friends upon his return to Iran show that Madani's criticism cuts both ways:

> I saw a country which was a land of wonders. It is
> said that Yankeeland has moved ahead of us a great
> deal. But I didn't see any progress. I suppose
> hundred-story buildings, pretty cars, nude dancing,
> parties day and night, subways, latest-model airplanes,

and spruced up ladies are signs of progress.[12]

He observes that having all this does not make a people civilized. In regard to freedom, he recalls his visit to the Statue of Liberty, which he defines as "freedom jailed on an island."[13]

In *Esmal in New York*, Madani displays an awareness similar to that of earlier writers, an awareness of the inevitable impact of the West on his country. Yet, even though on the surface and from the perspective of an uneducated character, he expresses the negative aspects of the West and Westerners, he is also aware of the positive features and generally, by implication, points out what can be learned and taken from the West to improve the conditions of his own society. A dilemma, in fact, seems to exist for Madani that had also existed for other writers before him, that is, how to approach the West and which aspects of Western culture should be accepted and which rejected.

This dilemma seems to permeate much of Persian fiction and is manifested in an ambivalence with regard to portraying Western characters and toward the Western cultural impact on Iran. Naser Taqva'i's well-crafted short story, "Aqa Julu" [Mr. Julu; translated into English as "Agha Julu"] (1965) serves as a revealing illustration of such ambivalence.[14]

"Mr. Julu" is the story of an Italian who arrives on a ship at Langeh, a small port town on the Persian Gulf, where he decides to reside for a time. Accustomed to foreign visitors from ships, the townspeople do not seem to regard him as an oddity at first, and even though some of the Shi'ite minority of the town, which is mostly populated by Sunnis, resist the Italian's attempts to become a part of the community, he eventually is accepted by the native population. Julio, the Italian visitor, is an engineer and initially is treated with some degree of awe and respect and is addressed as Mr. Engineer Julio. But, as he becomes a more familiar figure in the town, gradually all the titles are dropped from his name, in part because of Julio's ability and inclination to establish a bond of friendship with the children of the town, a tendency which lowers him in the eyes of the local adults. Nonetheless, Julio's time is spent as more than a playmate of the children. In fact, from the very onset of his arrival he begins a series of enterprises. He buys a truck to establish the first "freight company" in town, which he then sells, using the money to buy an old car to operate the first taxi service, and finally purchasing a camera and photographic equipment to open up the first photo studio in Langeh. Although these enterprises do not survive long, the town not being large enough to support them, Julio is never disillusioned. Gradually, he becomes accepted as a member of the community.

The side of Julio's character that attracts the children but at the same time causes him to be disliked by the adults is his carefree attitude toward life. Julio likes his drinking and singing, which he usually performs in the streets surrounded by a group of children. He is so well-liked by the children, who call him "Mr. Julu," that they actually prefer his company to their usual games and amusements.

Julio's drinking and carefree behavior cause concern in the townspeople, and since they seem to accept that he is there to stay, they decide to provide for him a wife, which also requires him to become a Moslem. This is, in fact, the beginning of the end for Julio. Gradually, the people become aware that although he has closed his photo studio, Julio has begun a new enterprise, taking nude pictures of his wife and selling them to the crews on the ships which occasionally anchor near Langeh. He continues this new business enterprise even after his first wife leaves him and he marries the daughter of the *kadkhoda*, or the official headman of the town. The story ends with the gendarmes coming to town and his arrest, even though he has destroyed all the evidence. According to one of the gendarmes, Julio has engaged in similar enterprises in various communities around the area.

"Mr. Julu" is a parable of sorts. The town and its people are a microcosm of Iran, and Julio is the outsider who comes to exploit its resources. However, the story suggests more than merely the Western exploitation of Iran. For one thing, although life goes on before the arrival of Julio in town, there is an air of stagnation and perpetual poverty over the townspeople, with no hope for the future. Julio's presence and his enterprises seem to stimulate activity, and even though his businesses fail one after another, at every turn he becomes the instigator of some change in the community. In one instance, he is able to engage a group of men in mining and in another, his presence challenges the porters to create a union. Then again, the Shi'ites and Sunnis put aside their own enmity toward each other to cooperate in finding a way to deal with Julio. Most significantly, the children are conscious of the dynamism that Julio brings with him to the town. For this reason, they continue to support him. Even in the end, despite the fact that some of them know of the nude photographs, one of the children helps him and surreptitiously removes the last picture that could be used as evidence against him from Julio's pocket.

Taqva'i's choice of an Italian as the Westerner, who is cast into the town from the sea, as it were, is a conscious one, one which allows him to avoid the pitfall of creating a character who might, from the very beginning, be condemned outright by the reader by the mere fact of the preconceived negative notions about the British or Americans. Instead, the focus of the story becomes the townspeople's reaction to the broader notion of change, which occurs as a result of the Western ideas and attitudes of Julio. On the one hand, his portrayal is negative, insofar as the character lacks sensitivity to the established norms and mores of the community. But on the other hand, he shows that the townspeople can learn, as do the children, a thing or two about how to live and enjoy life.

Even though the choice of the title and the focus of the plot on Julio make him the protagonist of the story, in terms of its relevance to its Iranian readers, "Mr. Julu" is an engaging study of the townspeople and how they cope with the changes that he effects on their community.[15]

Such reactions to and ability or lack thereof to adapt to change imposed by external factors is also the subject of Gholamhoseyn Sa'edi's *Tars va Larz* (1968) [translated into English as *Fear and Trembling*], which consists of six related stories all taking place in a small fishing village, an even smaller community than Langeh, on the Persian Gulf.[16] To one degree or another all the stories deal with the influence of external forces on the lives of the inhabitants, whether caused by superstitious beliefs or the disruption of their daily lives by some intruder. Of relevant concern to us in this discussion is the final story or episode of *Fear and Trembling*, in which the villagers discover one day that anchored near the village is a large ship, from which a small party of men, women, and servants come to shore with tents, equipment, and food to camp just outside the village. The initial reaction of the villagers to these intruders is one of curiosity combined with a degree of fear and apprehension. Nevertheless, gradually they overcome their fear, when for some unexplained reason the camping party decides to send a large quantity of food to the village people who have heretofore maintained a subsistence living. As the generosity of the visitors becomes a daily routine, the villagers eventually abandon their normal way of life. No longer in need of food, they do not find it necessary to continue the laborious task of fishing at sea and become totally dependent on the large amounts of food they receive from the visitors. As they become accustomed to the intruders, the villagers become more daring and begin to take various strange objects from the ship and the tents of the campers which they neither recognize nor are able to use. The now idle life of the villagers, who have nothing more to do than eat and become bloated, abruptly comes to an end one day when they discover that the ship and the campers have vanished. With the departure of the outsiders, the food supply ends, and the villagers, who have lost the ability to work and fish for their subsistence, panic. Faced with this new dilemma, they have even lost their ability to cope with the situation at hand. The scene on the day the villagers learn that the visitors have gone is revealing:

> A few days later the villagers started for the strangers' camp, holding hands, keeping an eye on one another. All were panting, too obese to take regular steps.
>
> "Hey, Zakariya! Hey, Kadkhoda! Look!" shouted Mohammad Ahmad Ali when they arrived near Salem Ahmad's house.
>
> The tents had been removed and there is no sign of the strangers on the shore.
>
> "What's happened?" said Mohammad Hajji Mostafa.
>
> "They seem to have left," said Kadkhoda.
>
> They turned and looked at the sea. It was empty. There was no sign of the ship or the launches.
>
> "Where have they gone?" said Kadkhoda.
>
> "I don't know," said Saleh.
>
> "I don't think they've left for good. I hope they'll come back," said Abd al-Javad.
>
> "What are we to do, if they don't?" said Mohammad Ahmad Ali.
>
> "I don't know," said Kadkhoda.
>
> "If they don't we're in a lot of trouble," said Zakariya.
>
> "Poor me, I'm worse off than anyone else here. At least you can go out to sea and fish. I can't do anything," said Zahed.
>
> "Not me, I'm not going to sea," said Saleh.
>
> "Me neither. I don't like fishing any more," said Abd al-Javad.

"I've gotten used to eating good stuff," said
Mohammad Ahmad Ali.

"I'm already hungry," said Kadkhoda.

"I want good food, good rich food," said Zakariya.

"I want variety. I don't like soup any more," said
Mohammad Ahmad Ali.

"Now that we can't have all kinds of food what
are we to do?" said Kadkhoda.

"Let's sit by the sea and wait. Maybe they'll come
back," said Mohammad Hajji Mostafa.

They started for the sea, moving their bloated
bodies with difficulty. The sea had shrunk. It had
ebbed away from the village and resembled a drying
swamp. The early morning sun rays were opaque gold
against the horizon. A foreign boat with a single black
sail wandered over the water, at a loss as to which
way to go.[17]

However, in contrast to earlier times, when with a sense of
community they worked together and helped one another, their
simple, tranquil life has been marred by hostility and
bloodthirstiness. Every villager tries to protect his own
possessions and steals from others whenever he can. The story
ends with one villager threatening the life of another for having
robbed him and still another, axe in hand, approaching the home
of a fellow villager in the dark of the night.

Even though Sa'edi never identifies the outsiders as
Westerners, and they are usually kept at a distance in the story
and only described in general terms, there are sufficient
indications in the story that they are, in fact, either Europeans
or Americans.[18] The image that he creates of these Westerners
is by no means negative insofar as their behavior or even
attitude toward the villagers is concerned. We simply see three
men and three women, not unlike Western vacationers, spending
their time leisurely on the shore, or in one instance visiting the
village out of curiosity and buying some odds and ends from the
villagers, who are enthusiastic to sell. In fact, although we read
the story from the perspective of the villagers, the Westerners
are, by comparison, portrayed in a more positive light, at least
on the surface, than are the villagers. Hence, not unlike
Taqva'i's "Mr. Julu," in this episode of *Fear and Trembling*, Sa'edi
does not fault the outsiders for the unfortunate consequences of
their visit. Rather, he appears to impugn the ignorance of the

villagers which makes them so susceptible to disaster when faced with changes brought about as the result of their willing, blind acceptance of what the Westerners have to offer them. In other words, Sa'edi seems neither to regard the West and Westerners as inherently evil nor advocate a blanket rejection of all things Western. As readers, we come away from the story with a sense of frustration, feeling that the fate of the villagers could have been different and their lives could, in fact, have taken a turn for the better had they only known how to take advantage of their brief encounter with their visitors. Nevertheless, there is a negative side to the Western characters which the story intimates, even if indirectly. Having been responsible for the villagers' abandoning their traditional ways of making a livelihood and having made them dependent upon them, the outside visitors in Sa'edi's story are neither aware of the unwanted changes resulting from their visit nor do they seem to be concerned about the fate of the people following their departure. The story in no way indicates any intentional ill will on the part of the Western visitors toward the villagers, but in a different sense, it presents them as insensitive to the consequences of their obvious generosity toward and visit to the village. The image of the Westerners that emerges from the story is one of ignorance, albeit of a different kind than that of the villagers.

Another example of the portrayal of Westerners as intruders into a peaceful, traditional community is Khosrow Shahani's "Borj-e Tarikhi" (1969) [translated into English as "The Historic Tower"], a satirical story about a small town in which the existence of an old tower has attracted the attention of a team of European archaeologists, headed by an aged Orientalist professor.[19]

As the narrator explains, before the arrival of the European archaeologists, no one had paid any particular attention to the tower, which seemed to them no different from any other nondescript site or object in the town. Since it was abandoned, flocks of birds had nested in its nooks and crannies, and the entrance to it had even been commonly used as a public toilet. In fact, it had become for the young hooligans a phallic symbol, with reference to which they would insult one another in quarrels. Once the European team visits the town to examine the tower and decides that it is indeed an ancient monument, suddenly the attitude of the townspeople toward the tower changes. They begin to take pride in it, as it now represents to them the glories of their past history. However, as the people gradually realize, more than mere pride and glory come with the recognition of the tower as a national monument. The tower is in need of maintenance and restoration, and funds must come from new taxes and higher prices.

The story ends when another team of archaeologists comes to examine the tower and decides that the tower is actually not very old at all and is, hence, not a significant monument of the ancient past. Once again, it becomes a nesting place for birds and a public toilet. What remains, however, are the new taxes and high prices. The old European Orientalist professor had made a mistake and is now searching in the Land of Darkness for the tower he thought he had found in the village.[20]

Cloaked in humor, Shahani's depiction of the Westerners in "The Historic Tower," not unlike Sa'edi's in *Fear and Trembling*, is not totally negative, although not altogether positive, either. As in *Fear and Trembling*, the Westerners are kept at a distance from the reader, who is not provided with a close-up picture of their character. In Shahani's story, the motivation of the Westerners in their intrusion into the quiet life of a small town, disturbing its traditional order, is somewhat clearer. The Orientalist professor wishes to make a name for himself, and, like the Westerners in Sa'edi's story, he appears oblivious to the effects of his "scholarly" encounter with the East.

Besides being oblivious to the effects of their brief visits on the lives of the native inhabitants, Westerners as portrayed in the stories discussed in this chapter seem also reluctant to try to understand them and learn about their existing ways, customs, and culture. In *Fear and Trembling*, the distance between the Westerners and Iranians is maintained, particularly by the Westerners, who seem to be interested only in whatever they find odd or exotic in their village. The only purpose of their visit, the story suggests, is to find and purchase odd, curious objects found in the villagers' households or to see the villagers' homes, which appear strange to them. In "The Historic Tower," a similar situation exists. The Orientalist professor and his archeological team are only interested in the monument and not at all in the inhabitants of the small town. And although Julio in "Mr. Julu" is portrayed as a Westerner who attempts to learn about the Iranians in Langeh, he is portrayed, on the one hand, as a marginal figure about town, not unlike a village idiot, and, on the other, as a man with an ulterior motive, namely making a profit through his various efforts to exploit the inhabitants.

Such a depiction of the Westerners as being reluctant to mingle and establish close ties with Iranians on a personal level perpetuates the gap between the Self and the Other, with the burden of blame placed mostly on the Westerners.

This gap and the writer's depiction of Westerners' attitude toward Iranians appears as a main theme of Simin Daneshvar's short story, "Eyd-e Iraniha" ["Iranian New Year"] (1961).[21] Daneshvar's story is a particularly interesting example of the attitude of Westerners toward Iranians since, unlike the other stories discussed so far, which are presented from an Iranian point of view, the perspective of "Iranian New Year" is that of Westerners, namely an American family, living in Tehran.

The story revolves around two small boys, John and Ted Michaelson, and their fascination with Haji Firuz, a minstrel-type character in blackface who appears on streets during the Iranian New Year holidays. One day, returning from school, the children see Haji Firuz in a red suit, cone-shaped hat and blackface standing on a street corner near their home. With great curiosity, they try to find out who he is and why he has made himself look as he does. The Haji Firuz character is often played by poor men who usually make their living around the neighborhood doing such odd jobs as cleaning pools in the summer and shoveling snow in winter. The New Year, in fact, provides them with an opportunity to make a little extra money singing and dancing in the streets. John and Ted soon learn that their Haji Firuz is the son of a shoeshine man in their neighborhood, and decide to furnish him with a new suit and hat. Furthermore, they also decide to build on a vacant, abandoned lot for Haji Firuz's father a shoeshine stall, which they decorate with magazine pictures of American presidents, Mickey Mouse, and football players, complete with an American flag over the stall door.

To these American children, Haji Firuz is merely a new source of amusement. Even their efforts, with the help of their mother, to make him a new outfit and to set up a shop for his father are presented in the story as part of their childish games. When they see Haji Firuz entertaining the people on the street, who occasionally throw him a small coin, the children, too, follow suit and take pleasure in the thought that they have provided him with the means to make a living. But as with all children's games, this one comes to an end one day when they find the shoeshine stall has been ruined in a rainstorm and later see Haji Firuz, whose new clothes are torn and soiled, following a "long wooden box," in fact, the coffin in which his father is being carried to the cemetery. Oblivious to the woeful situation of the man who plays Haji Firuz, the children are more upset about the clothes they have given him and the magazine pictures with which they had decorated the little shop, as one of them proposes to the other that they try to save the American flag which has gotten wet in the rain.

"Iranian New Year" can be interpreted as an allegory of the Iran of the late 1950s, when following the downfall of Prime Minister Mohammad Mosaddeq there were attempts by the United States to help Iran with its social reforms and economic development.[22] In this light, Daneshvar's story represents her own views and those of many other writers and intellectuals, and it stands as a commentary on the superficiality of such reforms and developments. For this reason, although presented from the perspective of the American children, as was pointed out, the story is once again a stereotypical depiction of these characters.

Given its anecdotal tone and one-dimensional characters, "Iranian New Year" fails as imaginative fiction. The characters are not developed fully enough to be plausible, nor does the story leave the reader with a lasting impression. The story is perhaps intended as a parable, in which Iranians and Americans are juxtaposed and the attitude of Americans toward Iran and the actual outcome of their actions are explained from the perspective of the author, the characters being in effect personifications of the writer's mental images of Westerners and the story a manufactured mirror serving the writer's objectives. In other words, the art of fiction itself is sacrificed in an effort to express the author's perceptions of the uninformed, misguided, and even arrogant attitude of the West toward Iran.[23]

Stories written by Iranian writers from the point of view of Westerners are not numerous in Persian fiction, and on the whole little attention is paid to the emotional and mental development of such characters. An exception is Sadeq Chubak's "Asb-e Chubi" [translated into English as "The Wooden Horse"], published in early 1966.[24]

"The Wooden Horse" is told from the perspective of a young French woman who has married an Iranian while he was a student in Paris. After six years of marriage and living in Iran for three years with her husband, Jalal, the woman spends her last few hours in Iran in an empty room alone with her small son on a cold Christmas night. Through her recollections, we learn how she and Jalal fell in love, married, and with their son came to Iran, where they were forced to submit to the wishes of Jalal's family, including remarrying in accordance with Islamic law. Through the eyes of the French woman, her impressions of the early days when she arrived at Jalal's parents' house, the sickening stench of the outhouse which seemed to dominate everything, the sickly appearance of Jalal's brothers and sisters, and later the death of Jalal's young sister from typhoid and her own contracting the disease and almost dying of it, a gloomy picture of Iranians and their society is presented. Worst of all, Jalal begins to change and eventually marries a fat, ugly cousin, abandoning his French wife and their son. With these memories, in stark contrast to those of her earlier days in France, both before she met Jalal and afterward, the woman has decided to leave, never to tell her son who his father is and never to look back on the nightmare she has suffered through for three years in Iran. The story ends with her tossing a wooden horse, bought by Jalal for the little boy, into the fire, thereby symbolically ridding herself of any memory of this bitter life experience.

Chubak's story may be a vehicle by which the author intends to show his Iranian readers more about themselves than about a Westerner, and in a sense, it is a form of social criticism more in line with much of his other work.[25] Nevertheless, even if inadvertently, he creates a more true-to-life Western character than do most other Iranian writers. Here, we neither have a stereotyped Westerner nor a symbolic representation of negative aspects of the West. Instead, Chubak gains the reader's sympathy for his protagonist and, rather than blaming the Westerner, puts her in the position of a victim of injustice. If anything, the stereotypical characters in the story are in fact the Iranians, before whom Chubak holds a Western mirror, as it were, and shows the Iranian readers some of the negative traits in their own society. The juxtaposition in this case may be an attempt to close the gap between the Self and the Other by reversing their roles, making the Self appear strange and the Other less so.

A writer who accomplishes this narrowing of the gap between the Self and the Other as regards the attitude of Iranians toward Westerners is Hushang Golshiri in his novella, "Jobbehkhaneh" ["The Antique Chamber"] (1983), and his novel *Keristin va Kid* [*Christine and the Kid*] (1971/1972).[26]

"The Antique Chamber" is the story of a one-night encounter of an Iranian college student with an eccentric couple. The husband is a white South African and the wife, a woman from an old, aristocratic Iranian family. The locale is Esfahan, a city which at the time of the story has many Western residents and visitors who have become a regular feature of the local scene.

The protagonist is a medical student who has chosen a quiet spot under a street lamp near the river to study for his examinations. But his studies are interrupted when a chauffeur-driven car appears with a mysterious woman inside who entices him into her car. Before long, the student finds himself in the woman's house, where he also meets her husband, Johnny.

The relationship between the husband and wife is somewhat reminiscent of that of George and Martha in Edward Albee's 1962 play, *Who's Afraid of Virginia Woolf?* Initially, the woman seems to have the upper hand. She orders her husband around, reprimands him for his actions, and beats him with a whip. She constantly makes fun of him and openly flirts with the student in front of him.

The reader is given the impression that the woman is trying to seduce the student to take revenge upon her husband, who regularly picks up prostitutes and brings them home, and has failed to be the ideal Western husband she had imagined he would be. After all, as a modern Iranian woman, she had expected that a Western man, unlike his traditional Iranian counterpart, would have a better understanding of and respect for women.

She recounts how she met Johnny in a bar in Johannesburg. Johnny had fallen in love with her and wanted to marry her. For this reason, he had brought his mother to introduce the Iranian girl to her. The mother, however, upon seeing her dark features, had thought that she was a mulatto, while Johnny had tried to explain to his mother that this was not so. "Believe me, Mother," Johnny had said to her, "she is not a mulatto. She is Iranian. She is of the Aryan race. And she is a princess."[27] The racial overtones in this and other scenes in the story show the student and the reader a different side of Johnny's character. He is not merely an innocent victim of the Iranian woman's mistreatment, but also the product of a racist and cruel culture, at least from the perspective of his wife, who recounts the incident. The evening passes in drunkenness with the student caught between the two, at a loss as to what to make of them. Later that evening, the woman takes the student to her bedroom.

Soon, however, Johnny begins to pound on his wife's bedroom
door, threatening to kill both of them with his revolver. "You
know about your law," he says. "You know that I can kill you
and no one will ever bother me for it."[28]   Half naked, his
clothes in hand, the student is forced to escape through the
window.   The story ends with the student running from the
dogs that guard the couple's courtyard garden and house and
arriving exhausted outside, where he reflects on his own
experience that night.   He finds a parallel between his own
situation and that of the political dissidents in their struggle for
independence against the government and foreign powers.   The
link that Golshiri establishes between the student's encounter
with the couple that night and the dissident's confrontation with
the Iranian authorities and Western powers, which has been
implicit, becomes explicit in the final pages.   The aristocratic
Iranian woman, or as we are reminded in the story several
times, the Iranian princess, is married to a man who represents
for the reader a Westerner, even though he is a South African.
They are both portrayed as ruthless people oblivious to the effect
they have on their victims.   In addition to the student, their two
servants are also caught up in the dangerous love-hate game
being played out between them.   In one scene, for instance,
Johnny tries to force Fatemeh, the maid servant, to drink vodka
and rips her clothes off while Rahim, the maid's husband, who
is the chauffeur and man-servant, is unable to intervene on
behalf of his wife.   Before escaping the student comes across
Rahim, whom he blames for helping the couple in their
dangerous games, and punches him in the face.   The servant can
only exonerate himself by saying, "I am innocent.   You can see
that I have a wife.   I have a wife and two children.   If I say
anything, if I interfere, they will kick me out."[29]   The student
is surprised to hear Rahim speak.   Unable to intervene in his
employer's actions, he has chosen to appear to be a deaf mute.

The political implications of the story become clear in the
end.   In a mental dialogue with his father, who had in his
younger days been involved in anti-government movements and
who has always warned his son against becoming involved in
such activities, the son reassures him:

I have always danced [to the tune of those in power],
Father; you told me yourself about the bear who is put
on a large hot copper frying pan to dance. And he
does. They beat the drums, blow the bugles, and the

bear dances. He jumps off one leg and lands on the other, leans on one leg and then the other, and sometimes moves his arms. And he moves his upper torso. He burns and moves. I have also danced, Father. Only danced. ... I am full of your quotations, of your advice, of your [Soviet broadcast] Peyk-e Iran Radio; I am full of peaceful coexistence, of the smell of burnt skin, of your whispering stories in my ears, of the tools of torture, made in the U.S.A., of the trade of powdered detergent for Russian weapons; of the presence of the head of the [Soviet] Politburo in the 2,500th Celebration of the [Iranian] Monarchy; of the thousands and thousands of Chinese girls carrying bouquets of flowers in His Majesty's retinue.[30]

The student understands that he, like the dancing bear, has been a torture victim. But more importantly, he realizes that, like other Iranians, he has been a victim of a strange marriage, which he terms "peaceful coexistence," between the rulers of his own country and the foreign powers, which even include the two powerful communist governments of the time.

Like Taqva'i in his short story "Mr. Julu," discussed earlier in this chapter, in "The Antique Chamber" Golshiri avoids choosing an American or an Englishman for his Western character. But, unlike the character of Julio, an Italian who does not necessarily represent to Iranians preconceived negative traits, as a white South African, Johnny in Golshiri's story would have immediately conjured up a hostile character for Iranian readers when the story was first written for adaptation as a feature film in 1974 and when it was rewritten and published in the early 1980s.[31] But Golshiri is not capitalizing on the negative image of a South African to create a stereotypical hostile character for his readers to hate. On the contrary, unlike the majority of Western characters that appear in Persian fiction, which are essentially presented superficially and often appear as cardboard characters, Johnny in "The Antique Chamber" is given a complex, tangible, fictional flesh and blood. There are, as we have discussed, elements of racism in his makeup, and he is at times cruel and appears to the student as an unfeeling brute. But Golshiri also adds to the depth of this character by describing him as a poet. On the one hand, his physical appearance connotes something animalistic about him, but on the other hand, his love of art and music and his obvious intellect display

him as not very different from the student observing him. In
other words, Golshiri's in-depth portrayal of Johnny and the
development of this character "humanize" him. It is in this
process of humanization of a Western character that the specter
of the Western character becomes a more familiar image with
which the reader can somehow identify, a process of
familiarization that helps narrow the gap between the Iranian
reader's Self and the Western Other in the form of a fictional
character. In *Christine and the Kid*, Golshiri had already explored
this process on a more personal level.

Partly because it followed Golshiri's highly acclaimed *Shazdeh
Ehtejab* (1968) [translated into English as *Prince Ehtejab*], which
captured a great deal of attention in Iran, *Christine and the Kid*
was not well received by critics.[32] Some even simply dismissed
it as a narcissistic account of its author's brief love affair with
an English woman and, therefore, unworthy of critical scrutiny.
Nevertheless, even if it is taken as an autobiographical story,
what critics failed to see in *Christine and the Kid* was the critical
self-analysis of its narrator, particularly with regard to the
British woman, as well as a demystification of the stereotyped
Western characters as inhumane beings devoid of feelings and
emotions. Unlike stories such as Jalal Al-e Ahmad's "The
American Husband," even the title of which reflects a
stereotypical view of Westerners, Golshiri's title projects a
humanization of his Western characters. This is true not only
with regard to Christine's name but also her husband's
nickname, "The Kid."

Christine and her husband, with their two small children, are
British nationals who live and work in the city of Esfahan. The
narrator becomes acquainted with the family through a friend,
Sa'id, a married man who has been having an affair with
Christine. The initial impressions left on the narrator before he
actually gets to know the British family are not in some respects
different from Esmal's judgments of the morality of American
women in Madani's *Esmal in New York*, discussed earlier in this
chapter. The narrator of Golshiri's story also sees Christine and
her husband as people with loose morals, since both have
regular affairs outside their marriage, each aware of those of the
other. Eventually, the narrator also enters the picture, and
gradually his relationship with the family develops into a love
affair with Christine. Although as a writer the narrator attempts
to remain a mere observer, even in his relationship with
Christine, he begins to see the British family as individuals with

each of whom he establishes some sort of bond. Also, through them he begins to gain a degree of awareness of his own self and the individuality of each member of the family. At the same time, by introducing other characters, both Iranian and Western, into his story, Golshiri is able to close the gap between the Iranian Self of the narrator and the British "otherness" of Christine. The narrator, whose purpose in befriending the British family has been to learn English, gradually realizes, for instance, that the British, too, are no strangers to suffering, that they also have words for screaming and shrieking from pain:

> Shriek. It is a good word. So they have it too; they have also shrieked, and they can understand it. I am talking about all the Britishers. In fact, people have shrieked all over the world. I must ask a Russian what the word is for shrieking and also my friend who knows French well. The Chinese symbol for it must be strange: a few short and long syllables, exactly like shrieking, like the sound of shrieking. Weeping. The word for weeping is simple, soft, two syllables. Like quiet, eternal sobbing, like when we are drunk, or weep and pretend that we are drunk.[33]

Language itself is an important factor in creating barriers between the Self and the Other. Once linguistic barriers begin to break down, the gap narrows and the Other, in the mind of the observer, begins to assume the more human characteristics of the Self. By this time, the narrator has learned enough of the language of the Other to understand that a phrase such as "shut up," for instance, is not as offensive as he had once thought. He also comes to the realization that he cannot blame an individual for the past acts of others of the same nationality:

> What was the use of teasing her? To ask her, for example, Have you heard of Reuter, or d'Arcy, for instance, or Colonel Smyth or even James Morier, or any other damn name? After all, what does it have to do with them? They are among us like a lone island. Or [what does it have] to do with the children? ... They don't even know a word of Persian, and when they go back to their own island, they are sure to forget.[34]

Given the nature of modernist literature, with its emphasis on the individual, it is inevitable for a modernist writer such as Golshiri to break the tradition of stereotypical representation of Westerners and with it the prejudice against the stereotyped British. Hence, his Western characters are portrayed as individuals who stand for themselves, not for a certain image of Westerners in general that exists in the Iranian psyche. In contrast to much of Iranian fiction, such as Iraj Pezeshkzad's *My Dear Uncle Napoleon*, in which the writer satirizes his generation's Anglophobia, and Madani's *Esmal in New York*, in which the author at least inadvertently instills in the reader's mind similar sentiments toward the Americans, in *Christine and the Kid*, Golshiri does not perpetuate the negative image of the West and Westerners, nor does he present a more positive image at the expense of criticizing Iranians and their society. He simply constructs a world in which human beings are viewed by each other as individuals and relate to each other accordingly.

6 POST-REVOLUTIONARY REFLECTIONS

The perpetual conflict between the guardians of tradition and the proponents of change has undoubtedly influenced the images of the West and Westerners in the mirror of the Iranian psyche as reflected in Persian fiction. While negative images of the West have been in many instances a reaction to Western-style changes that were seen as a threat to the traditional way of life in Iran, the positive images have been the product of the minds of those who advocated the restructuring of the society through social, political, economic, scientific, and technological progress and change. To this, however, the political factor in its various forms must also be added as an element that has affected the images of the West and Westerners, particularly in the present century.[1]

To some extent the examples discussed in all the previous chapters, and to a greater degree those presented in Chapters 4 and 5, are intended to show how perceptions of Iranian writers have been affected by the behavior and actions of Western powers, particularly in connection with Iran. The reactions of writers in such stories as *The Braves of Tangestan, My Dear Uncle Napoleon, The School Principal, Savushun, Fear and Trembling,* and "The Historic Tower" are largely based on a sense of patriotism, displayed either explicitly or implicitly in these stories. At the same time, modern Persian fiction since its beginnings in the late nineteenth century has functioned for its authors as a medium through which to express dissatisfaction with the ruling apparatus and the political regime in power, which has been viewed by many Iranians as a puppet government and an instrument of Western powers.

During the Pahlavi regime, the open expression of a linkage between the governing regime or the royal court and dominant Western powers was avoided. Government-imposed censorship controlled and prevented such expressions in print or any other medium of public communication.² Nevertheless, criticism of the West without linkage to the Pahlavi regime could be found in abundance and was even sanctioned at times by the regime in power. A nonfictional example of such a critical portrayal of the West is Ehsan Naraqi's *Ghorbat-e Gharb* [*The Alienation of the West*], which was published first in 1974 and went through at least four printings prior to the Islamic Revolution.³ In it the author, who has had extensive experience living in the West and is intimately familiar with Western societies, presents a very negative view of these societies and cultures. He sees a West that is suffering from a series of social and spiritual crises. Unlike some earlier Iranian intellectuals who advocated for Iran total emulation of the West, he proposes that Iran and other Eastern countries learn from the mistakes of the Westerners and build "another culture" for the future.⁴

The West that Naraqi presents faces a crisis because, firstly, in emphasizing increased economic production and satisfying the material necessities of life, the West has ignored emotional and spiritual needs. Subsequently, lack of attention to family life has resulted in problems such as loneliness and alienation. Secondly, as a result of excessive reliance on technology, the West faces an ecological crisis. Thirdly, technology has brought about a situation in which human liberties have been restricted, and indeed man himself has become a slave to the machine. Finally, consumerism, bureaucracy, and mechanized systems have reduced man to a being with no remaining initiative of his own; the machine controls justice, freedom, democracy and welfare.⁵

Such criticism of the West is essentially cultural and by no means new, as it appears in the works of many Iranian writers and thinkers throughout the nineteenth and twentieth centuries. Perhaps the most prominent and outspoken of such thinkers was Ahmad Kasravi (1890–1946), who had already expressed similar views in his polemical writings and speeches several decades earlier. In his 1933 book called *A'in* [Creed], Kasravi expresses his anxiety about the dire conditions in the world and states that "the path Europe has chosen for life ... will have sinister consequences." The world created by the Europeans, according to him, has an orderly, beneficial facade, but "the people of that world lack tranquility and happiness."⁶ In regard to Naraqi's notion that man has become a slave to the machine, as well, Kasravi had previously expressed his concerns, essentially considering the industrialization of the West as the cause of unemployment and the increase in the gap between the "haves" and "have nots" in those societies. Likewise, Naraqi's concerns about the West and its disregard for the spiritual and emotional needs of human beings had already been expressed frequently by Kasravi. In fact, what Naraqi expresses in his *The Alienation of the West* in the garb of sociological or socio-cultural polemics is in many ways a reiteration of the concerns expressed by Kasravi and others in various forms for more than a century.[7]

As stated earlier, despite the existence of censorship throughout the Pahlavi period, the expression of critical views about the West was not only tolerated but, for a variety of politically expedient reasons, even at times provided with a forum. It is in keeping with the same government policy that allowed, and perhaps even encouraged, the expression of negative aspects of Western culture in Persian fiction, provided that it did not involve direct criticism of the Iranian regime itself. Many anti-regime writers, however, with their negative portrayal of aspects of Western culture and characters in their work, were also criticizing, particularly in the two or three decades prior to the Islamic Revolution, the regime of Mohammad Reza Shah Pahlavi, which was commonly regarded as pro-Western.

With the 1978–1979 Islamic Revolution and the overthrow of the Pahlavi dynasty, there was no longer any obstacle for Iranian writers in speaking and writing openly about the connections between the Pahlavi regime and the Western powers, and even identifying the shah and his government as their agents in Iran. The anti-Western slogans of the revolutionaries and the revolutionary government since the beginning of the Islamic upheaval in Iran were in themselves clear enough signals to writers to now openly express their anti-Western political views in fictional and nonfictional forms, and also to blame the West for the atrocities of the overthrown dictatorial regime and its feared SAVAK secret police in addition to the threats to the Iranian and Islamic traditional values and way of life that the "Westernized shah" had brought about.

Among the writers who have taken advantage of the anti-Western climate in Iran since the revolution to write novels that focus particularly on the direct influence of the American government on the Iranian military and secret police is Reza Baraheni, a noted literary critic who had also published poetry and fiction prior to the revolution. For Baraheni, who had published two books in English in the United States during his residence abroad in the 1970s, direct criticism of the Pahlavi regime and specifically its SAVAK secret police was nothing new.[8]   The revolution, however, provided him with the opportunity to write, and in some cases rewrite, his stories about the lives of Iranian intellectuals and their dealings with the Pahlavi regime for a wider Iranian audience and thereby "expose" the extent of the involvement of the Western powers, particularly the United States, in the day-to-day affairs of the Iranian government.   Already in his *Avaz-e Koshtegan* [*The Song of the Slaughtered*], published in 1983, but according to the author written in 1974 and 1975, Baraheni had dealt with the relationship between the Iranian secret police and American agents.[9]

   The Song of the Slaughtered is the story of Mahmud Sharifi, a university professor, who is arrested and tortured by the secret police because his writings contain anti-government implications. During an interrogation in which the secret police are trying to determine whether or not he is the author of certain letters written in English and mailed to Europe, we find in attendance an American agent, a handwriting expert, who is well aware of the ruthlessness of the Iranian secret police, and in fact aids them in their dealings with the political opponents of the regime. Baraheni finds no need to develop the character of the American agent in this novel.   The purpose here is merely to show that Americans not only knew about but were involved in the actions of the feared SAVAK security apparatus.   In his later novel, *Razha-ye Sarzamin-e Man* [*The Mysteries of My Homeland*] (1987), however, Baraheni not only delves quite extensively into the issue of American governmental involvement in and control over the affairs of Iran but also finds an opportunity to present to his reader a variety of American characters.[10]

   Temporally, *The Mysteries of My Homeland* spans the late 1950s to early 1980s.   The locale is for the most part the northwestern province of Azarbaijan, on the Soviet border, where American military and intelligence services have stationed their personnel for the surveillance of Soviet activities across the border and the training of the Iranian military in preparation for a potential Soviet attack.   The novel takes the form of a series of third-person narratives and first-person monologues by various characters.   The Americans are all military and intelligence officials, and the Iranians as well are either military or intelligence officials, interpreters to American personnel, or the occasional civilian somehow involved in their affairs.

The story opens in winter on a road from Tabriz to Tehran. An American sergeant accompanied by his Iranian interpreter is driving in a military truck, and although there have been warnings that a severe snowstorm is underway and will make traveling extremely hazardous, the sergeant decides to go on, since the American personnel in the region have been ordered not to spend the night anywhere on the road. The sergeant soon realizes that he should have heeded the warning, since before long the truck is caught in the snowstorm, and the two travelers are forced to spend the cold night in a desolate area.

This opening chapter sets the tone for the remainder of the 1,300-page novel. It introduces to the reader a foreshadowing of the many American characters which appear throughout the story. Unlike many Iranian writers whose fictional representations of Americans are essentially cardboard characters based on their vague perceptions of Westerners, Baraheni's American characters are more true-to-life. Nevertheless, he models these characters after a general stereotypical image, variations on the so-called "Ugly American." The attitude of Iranians toward these American characters can be seen in the relationship between the interpreter and Davis, the American sergeant, who is described as a man who was "neither good, nor bad. On the whole, he was a coward. Out of simplemindedness, he asked the interpreter question after question."[11] Davis' questions and the interpreter's answers reveal not only the image that Baraheni attempts to create of the American characters in his novel, but also the climate of distrust and tension that exists throughout the story between the Iranians and Americans.

"Why are the Tabriz prostitutes disinclined to make love to Americans?" Davis asks, to which the interpreter replies, "I have no idea. You'll have to ask them." He further wants to know why they were willing to sleep with the Russians during the occupation of Tabriz by the Red Army. With this, Davis is trying to give a political dimension to the attitude of the prostitutes toward the Americans and the Russians. The response of the interpreter is disingenuous but revealing: "I have no idea. Besides, you had better exclude the Tabriz prostitutes from participating in the Cold War between the Eastern and Western blocs."[12] The interpreter then suggests that the fact that some of the Russian soldiers spoke Turkish, their common language, with the prostitutes might have been the reason for their better treatment. Davis' response becomes uncharacteristically polemical:

> Or perhaps there is the issue of nation, nationality,
> and such nonsense. Besides, you accuse me of
> including the prostitutes in the Cold War while you
> are involving them in the issue of language and
> nationalism. In my opinion, a prostitute is just a
> prostitute and is always concerned with a man's
> money, not his language and nationality.[13]

The interpreter then argues that race and nationality play an important part in such relations, as Davis confesses that if he had to choose between a white and a black prostitute he would choose the former. Their argument ends with Davis accusing the interpreter and Iranians in general of having their umbilical cord tied to Moscow. The interpreter's defense against the implication of being labeled a communist is:

> In Iran, whenever someone expresses dislike for
> Americans or the government, he is immediately told
> that his umbilical cord is tied to Moscow. What
> does a discussion about the Tabriz prostitutes have to
> do with Moscow? My umbilical cord is tied to one
> place, and that is Tabriz.[14]

Further on in the same chapter, another conversation takes place between Davis and the interpreter, in which Baraheni seeks to further explore the image of the Ugly American. Stuck in the middle of the snow-covered road, feeling quite lonely and helpless, and especially worried about a wolf that has been following them, Davis remarks: "It is in such places that one really feels that one is far away from America. Once in Korea, in the trenches when I was wounded, I felt that I was not in America. And now here as well."[15] Then, in response to the interpreter, who declares, "Do not be afraid, we Iranians lack the zeal that the Koreans possess," Davis states: "Make no mistake. In Asia, if you put a gun in the hand of anyone, he will first try to get rid of the Americans." He then adds: "I have no doubt about it. ... The sparkle in the eyes of the Korean and the anger in the eyes of the Iranian villagers are both like the firing squad to me."[16] Nevertheless, despite the fear that Davis has of non-Westerners, Baraheni uses a cliche that stereotypes him as an American. In Davis' words, "America is wherever an American sets his foot."[17]

The stage having been set for confrontation between these characters from two cultures against the backdrop of the merciless elements of nature, where they are so isolated that it appears "as if they had returned to the primitive man," the narrator pontificates on their differences:

> What was it that differentiated these two from one
> another? Not having a common identity and
> belonging to two different nations with separate
> histories and traditions? One being a military man
> and the other a civilian? The fact that the interpreter
> belonged to an oppressed people and the American
> to a domineering government? They were both alone
> against this snowy night, but they were also alone
> against each other. ... Under such circumstances, the
> psychological and individual differences between
> these two persons are not that important. What
> separated them was something greater, more general,
> more global.[18]

The differences between these two characters are, therefore, the differences between the broader Iranian Self and the American Other. And although Baraheni is careful not to create flat characters in this and other episodes of his novel, these and many of the characters that he introduces later assume symbolic roles. Within this context, he also creates a symbolic and folkloric fate for the American sergeant.

When the interpreter wakes up the next morning, he finds the eyes of a frightening wolf staring through the windshield of the truck. After waking his companion, who makes an effort to scare the wolf away by shooting at him, the interpreter is forced by Davis to go to the nearby village for help. The wolf seems to be no threat to the interpreter. It is, we learn, a legendary wolf known as the "Killer of Foreigners." When he returns with a number of villagers, he finds that Davis has been killed by the wolf. The villagers are not at all surprised, because this strange beast has killed other foreigners, including a Russian Cossack and a British colonel, in the past. The reason for this strange phenomenon is explained by an old villager: "When we become helpless and none of us are able to do anything, the sense of honor of the 'Killer of Foreigners' is provoked."[19]

The first episode of *The Mysteries of My Homeland*, as stated above, sets the tone for the remainder of the novel. Various aspects of the character of Davis as well as his relationship with Iranians and their attitude toward Americans are developed in the characters and episodes that follow.

One such character, Captain Crosley, a senior American military adviser in Iran, is an expansion of the image of the Ugly American, particularly in his relationship with an Iranian officer, Colonel Jazayeri. In contrast to Colonel Jazayeri, a short, unkempt, and timid man, Captain Crosley is a tall, robust giant of a man whose face seems to represent the "red and white totality of American civilization," who would show off his "handsome and clean-shaven face, with all the vitamins that seemed to ooze out of the pores and cells of his skin" to the Colonel, to the Iranian military regiment, and to the townspeople.[20]

An unspoken tension develops between these two men, who represent two cultures with differing outlooks on life. The Iranian colonel's interests lie chiefly in his lovebirds, pigeons, canaries, and cat, and in his opium smoking and mystical thoughts. He is usually unshaven, a habit that clearly perturbs Captain Crosley and which becomes a bone of contention between them. The American advisor takes every opportunity to scold the Iranian officer for not having shaved, and the Iranian colonel, who believes that "although the Americans have not occupied Iran, they cannot live without the feeling of occupying other countries," nurtures the wish, it would appear, to "avenge their occupation, subjugation, colonialization, coup d'etat, and the presence of the superior race" by maintaining his unshaven appearance.[21] The condescending behavior of the American captain, with his sense of superiority, and the Iranian colonel's wounded pride and sense of inferiority ultimately collide and explode. A group of soldiers who have been witness to this relationship, not unlike the wolf in the previous section, with the Colonel's tacit approval, kill the foreigner. In retaliation for the assassination of Captain Crosley, however, more than a dozen Iranian military men, including the Colonel, are executed.

In the portrait of Captain Crosley, Baraheni proffers a very dubious image of the American character, much reminiscent of the widespread image of the American soldier in Vietnam, who is merciless, ethnocentric, unfeeling, and suffering from psychological disorders, but who is also feeling a twinge of conscience. Captain Crosley appears to be an embodiment of many traits—racism, violence, and cruelty—that instill hatred of Americans in the hearts of their victims. The Iranian colonel is certain that the "Captain has left the United States to come abroad to impose his will on others."[22] To the Colonel, who "had surely read about American democracy and about the religious beliefs of most Americans," not only is the Captain's existence "in contradiction to all his ideas and suppositions about American democracy, but even through the Captain, he found the American God to be in violation of divine justice."[23] Baraheni provides sufficient evidence in his portrayal of the Captain to justify such a characterization by the Colonel and other Iranian characters, as well as his readers. Captain Crosley is violent by nature, even beating the prostitutes that he demands to have in various towns to which he travels around the province. In his opinion, the Iranian government pays all his expenses, including the prostitutes' fees, so that he can teach the Iranian army to prevent the communist neighbors to the north from gaining access to the Persian Gulf. He describes the American foreign policy to his interpreter, stating that if Americans would not prepare Iranians to defend themselves:

> War would break out. The Russians would reach
> Tehran in one day. In another few days, they would
> reach Khuzestan Province and the Persian Gulf.
> They would change the name of the Persian Gulf to
> Lenin Lake. The Russians have always wanted
> access to the warm waters. And you cannot blame
> them for that. All the nations in the northern
> hemisphere want to have access to the tropical
> regions. We are also moving south; we want the
> whole of Central and Latin America. Since the time
> of Peter the Great, the Russians, too, have wanted to
> reach the warm waters. For a while, they were
> feeling really cold. And they have been feeling cold
> since the Bolshevik Revolution, even colder than
> before. They want the warm waters, and then they
> will take over all of the oil in Iran and the Arab
> countries. Do you know what would happen then?
> The world would become cold and dark. In a few
> years, civilized Europe would turn into a
> wasteland.[24]

While Captain Crosley represents the negative image of the

American in this novel, Baraheni provides us with a brief glance at another stereotypical picture of Americans as well, in Captain Douglas, an army reservist whose non-military profession is teaching literature. Unlike Crosley, Captain Douglas expresses dislike for the European and American cultures, with all their institutions. On the other hand, he is fascinated by the Iranians, particularly the people of Tabriz, because of their pristine, "biblical" way of life:

> You Tabrizis lead a primitive life. Your attitudes are
> the attitudes of the Old Testament. Even though
> your life is Islamic, in every corner of Azarbaijan, I
> see behavior, I see relations that call to mind the Old
> Testament. The faces of the old men call to mind
> Noah, Abraham, Moses, Jacob, and Daniel. ... Your
> old women on the banks of the rivers, as they sit
> and wash clothes, and the children with their runny
> noses, with their distended stomachs and hazel eyes,
> are the characters of the Holy Book. There is
> poverty; there is trachoma; there are the bloated
> bellies of the children suffering from malnutrition;
> and certainly there is robbery, crime, and perversion.
> But the girls with hazel and honey-colored eyes in
> Mahabad, Ardabil, Zanjan and Jolfa who carry jugs
> of water from the spring on their shoulders are like
> the future wives of the prophets in the Old
> Testament.[25]

To the Iranian interpreter listening to Captain Douglas' pontification, Douglas is one side of the American coin, of which Crosley is the other. His words in response may very well be the author's own:

> You are a romantic American, escaping from your
> own era to ours, and from our era to another, to the
> bygone era of history. The people here, like
> everywhere else, are made of skin, bone, flesh,
> brains, instincts, emotions, and thoughts. You
> Americans look at people in two ways. One is like
> Captain Crosley, who thinks everything and everyone
> is an instrument for his own gratification, and
> another is like you, who, because he is appalled by
> his own civilization, idealize us and see our poor

girls, who have to carry drinking water several kilometers to their homes because they have no running water, as the future wives of Hebrew prophets. One kills to stay alive, and the other, that is, you, embraces his object so tightly that the victim is either suffocated by excessive closeness and love or is metamorphosed into another creature altogether.[26]

The Douglases of Baraheni's novel, however, are few. The only other notable example appears later in the story, during the revolution, when upon the departure of the shah from Iran, an American in the crowds shouts "Death to the Shah," and the people cheer him, kiss him, and carry him on their shoulders in the demonstrations. On the other hand, the image of the Crosleys dominates the story. The most important of these figures is Biltmore, a cold-blooded intelligence officer in charge of the interrogation and execution of Crosley's killers. For several years Biltmore engages in the infiltration and control of the Iranian military and secret police and also recruits Iranians to spy for the United States. His relationship with an influential Iranian general and his wife takes on a symbolic meaning in the novel. The general, who cannot have children, asks Biltmore to make love to his wife—because he wishes to have a child by an American—and to himself, having had many such relations with countless young men. Eventually the love triangle between Biltmore, the general, and his wife comes to represent, as Biltmore writes, the "warm relations between the Americans and the shah's military."[27] The relationship between the United States intelligence service and military and their Iranian counterparts as well as the American influence over and control of the shah and his government become the primary subject matter of the remainder of Baraheni's novel, which continues up to the Islamic Revolution and even beyond. Most of the Iranians who have served the Americans are punished in various ways, as are the main American players in the story. Later, we find Biltmore in post-war Vietnam, where he dies after having gone mad. The Iranian general is murdered by one of his victims, in fact, his wife's brother, who has become an American spy and continues his activities on behalf of the American government for some time after the revolution. The general's wife and her brother are eventually arrested and executed by the revolutionary government.

America and Americans in Baraheni's novel represent an imperialist power and its agents, who seem to lack any human traits in their dealings with their victims. The America of Baraheni is the U.S. government, and the American people are merely its instruments.

In his effort to expose the American involvement in Iran and its control over the Iranian government, Baraheni is undoubtedly reiterating the notions about America that have existed in many other countries in the post–Vietnam war era. These notions were reinforced in Iran in the anti-American climate of the Islamic Revolution. On one level, the presentation of such a monolithic image of America and Americans is intentional, motivated by the writer's own political views and those of many of his compatriots who had just been through the experience of living under a dictatorship which they blamed on Westerners in general and Americans in particular. In some respects Baraheni may display a degree of naivete in presenting such a stereotypical view of America, despite the fact that he has experienced a relatively intimate knowledge and understanding of the West. But it should also be kept in mind that such a portrayal serves, perhaps consciously, a political purpose and is, hence, inevitably black and white, good and evil.

On another level, novels such as *The Mysteries of My Homeland* serve a therapeutic purpose. Sentiments that had been suppressed during the Pahlavi regime, particularly since the fall of the government of Dr. Mohammad Mosaddeq in 1953, suddenly find release with the Islamic Revolution. For the Iranian masses in the streets, they are expressed in cries of "Death to America" and the burning of the American flag. They find expression with the leader of the revolution in calling America "The Great Satan," and for his young zealot supporters in occupying the American Embassy in Tehran and taking hostages, in regarding the embassy as a "Spy Nest" and the diplomats as spies. And for the fiction writer, those sentiments that had been bottled up for decades are released in the form of fictional images of America and Americans.

But Baraheni and other Iranian writers who have lived in Iran and who were overwhelmed by the revolutionary climate were not unique in their portrayal of America as a ruthless, imperialist power and Americans as its agents. In his first novel, *Cry for My Revolution, Iran*, Manoucher Parvin, who has lived in the United States most of his life, creates characters and situations reminiscent of those of Baraheni.[28]

Written in English and for an American audience, *Cry for My Revolution, Iran* is the story of the activities of anti-Pahlavi Iranian students in the United States and covers the same time frame as Baraheni's novel, that is, the two or three decades prior to the Islamic Revolution. Parvin's novel, like Baraheni's, is therapeutic for the writer and many like-minded Iranians of his generation, particularly activist Iranian students who lived abroad in Europe and America. Although his portraits of American characters in the novel may be stereotypical, Parvin does not present all of his Western characters as evil. Nevertheless, the image of Americans that emerges from his novel is essentially no different from the one that is portrayed in *The Mysteries of My Homeland*. Told essentially from the perspective of Professor Pirooz, an Iranian who has lived and worked in the United States for many years, the story revolves around the lives of Ali, Sara, and Eric. Ali is the romantic revolutionary hero of the novel, who falls in love with Sara, a fellow student at Columbia University. Their mutual collegemate, Eric, is the arch-villain of the novel who leads the pro-government, counterrevolutionary demonstrations at the University, and after graduation becomes a CIA agent. Sara becomes pregnant by Ali, who, unaware of Sara's condition, returns to Iran to fight against the shah's regime. Eric, who also has a romantic interest in Sara, proposes marriage, which she feels obliged to accept. A few years later, during the Islamic Revolution, Eric, Sara, and her son are in Iran, Eric having become the CIA station chief in Iran, working with the shah's SAVAK agents to suppress anti-government groups, among whom Ali has now become a major figure. The fate of the American arch-villain in Parvin's novel is not unlike the fates of those of Baraheni's novel. Parvin's punishment for Eric in the novel is to have him commit suicide. Ali too is killed, not by the shah's government, but later by the Islamic regime. Sara, who has now become enlightened about Ali's selflessness and self-sacrifice and the evils of her own government, represented by Eric, is fortunate enough to escape the chaos of the revolutionary climate in Iran and return to the United States with her son.

In an afterword to the novel, Parvin unabashedly explains that the "characters of this novel stand for themselves, but they are also symbols." While Ali represents "the unknown altruistic revolutionary," Sara symbolizes the "part of America which is sensitive and wants to learn." Eric, on the other hand, stands for that part of America that "considers the U.S. always right and believes might makes right." Moreover, "the CIA stands for the force of darkness overseeing virtually all of the 'free world.'"[29]

Open expression of the linkage between the Pahlavi regime and Western powers in the fiction published after the revolution finds its way even into stories that would otherwise have been apolitical, or at least unrelated to international politics. *Raqs-e Ranj* [The Dance of Suffering] (1981), by Khosrow Nasimi, is the story of the family of a small farmer driven off his land and out of his village by a merciless landlord.[30] The tragic fate of this family is blamed not only on the shah's land reform program and his government in general, but on the Western powers as well. After being forced to migrate to the city, the family of Rahman, a hardworking farmer, falls apart. His wife becomes a prostitute, and after years of suffering and doing odd jobs, he joins a revolutionary group at the onset of the Islamic upheaval. The connection between this individual tragedy and the hands of Western imperialists is established for the reader even before he or she begins the story, in an introduction written by the noted writer and translator, Mohammad Qazi:

> The fascist regime of the Pahlavi dynasty, in its fifty-five years of dictatorial rule, was responsible for much injustice to the nation and the destruction of many families. Reza Khan [Reza Shah], who was the agent for carrying out the policies of the colonialist government of Great Britain, not only imprisoned all the freedom-loving, patriotic, and compassionate intellectuals of our homeland in the dark dungeons of Qasr Prison and the deadly places of exile, where they either rotted away or were killed, not only did he cut out their tongues and break their legs, but ... usurped the people's land ... and planned to take possession of all agricultural and other property throughout Iran as his own. But the breeze of freedom that blew with the storm of World War II did not allow him to complete and carry out his sinister plan and overthrew him.
>
> However, [Western] imperialism was not and will not be sitting idly by. It is ever hungry for the blood of the workers and laborers of the whole world. This time, the heir of colonialism, the world-

devouring America, imposed its son, Mohammad
Reza, to rule over the lives and property of our
suffering and oppressed people.[31]

Further on, Qazi observes that Mohammad Reza Pahlavi's
land reform program was merely a propaganda ploy of plunder
by the regime which resulted in the destruction of farmers and
farming and "dependence on U.S. imperialism and its puppets,
even for wheat and daily bread."[32]

The shadow Qazi casts over the entire novel with his
introduction slants our reading of the story to such a degree that
the tragic fate of Rahman's family is blamed not only on the
shah but indirectly on U.S. imperialism, even though Nasimi's
novel itself contains few expressions of such sentiments. In the
final pages of the story, however, when asked by another
revolutionary whether he is a Bakhtiari tribesman (intimating
that he possesses a nomadic, free spirit), Rahman's response
explicitly reveals the imperialist shadow of the West, which
parallels the viewpoint expressed by Qazi, as if the novel were
written after the introduction and the novelist has found an
opportunity to express such sentiments openly through his
protagonist. In answer to his friend, Rahman sighs and says:

> There are no Bakhtiari tribesmen left anymore. They
> were all castrated, either by the British or the
> Americans. They now either want to work for the
> oil company or SAVAK.[33]

The West and the shah's regime, as oppressive forces
against which the revolutionaries rebel, become indistinguishable.
Revolutionary slogans against these forces are often combined
and shouted in the same breath. In a small collection of short
stories, *Bargha'i az Fasl-e Khun* [Leaves from the Season of Blood]
(1980), by Faramarz Talebi, which chronicles the lives and
activities of young students during the revolutionary uprising,
students shout slogans or repeat statements they have heard in
which America and the shah or shah's regime are used
synonymously, or at least cursed in the same breath:

> Akbar no longer thinks about work. He no longer
> thinks about the bad conditions of the house. Now
> he can even tolerate the empty supper cloth. ... [He
> thinks about] the street demonstrations, about the

slogans he shouted against the shah with his
clenched fists, shouts against the shah's soldiers and
against America.[34]

In another slogan, the adjective used to describe the shah
expresses the notion that the shah and America are regarded as
one and the same: "This [pro-]American shah must be executed
before the nation." And still another: "Army, you belong to us,
not to America."[35] In a revolutionary handout that students
distribute, as one student explains to another, the identification
of the hostile image of the shah with America is thus explained:
"In these handouts, we want to tell the people that the shah's
regime is so dependent on the United States that we must not
only drive the shah out, but we must also get rid of America."
Hence they write on walls: "Say, Death to the Shah, say, Death
to America, the supporter of the shah, the executioner."[36]
Talebi's brief chronicle of the revolution, with its anti-
shah/anti-American slogans, is in turn another revolutionary
pamphlet, a revolutionary slogan, as it were, written at the
height of the anti-American climate of the early 1980s in Iran.
In other words, it functions both as a device at the service of the
revolution and also a record of the ongoing events. There is a
conviction on the part of the author that his stories are also
recorded history. The America which is thus portrayed is the
America of Islamic revolutionary slogans. This is the America
that is also found in Ali Kamali's *Enqelab* [*Revolution*].[37]
Published in 1979, *Revolution* is described by its author as
the "oral literature" and "history" of the revolution up to mid-
May of 1979. The author has essentially collected slogans,
rhymes, jokes, and songs that were heard on the streets or
written on placards carried by revolutionaries or on walls. On
virtually every page of this collection of some 550 pages,
whether in songs and slogans against the shah and his regime
or in support of Ayatollah Khomeini and the revolution, there
are pejorative references to the United States and occasionally
other Western powers. The image of America and the West in
general that emerges from these statements is that of an abstract
enemy, a sinister force that supports the dictatorial regime of the
shah and his SAVAK secret police.
The effect of such an abstract, negative image of the West
on the general populace in Iran is so pervasive and so
overpowering that it allows little opportunity for
writers—particularly those who sympathize with the overall

direction of the revolution and are therefore more susceptible to public sentiments—to escape becoming victims of it and recreating this image in their fiction.   Nonetheless, there are writers who did not readily submit to the prevalent anti-Western climate and who display a degree of caution in their portrayal of the West and Western characters.   Mahshid Amirshahy belongs to just such a group of Iranian writers of fiction.

Amirshahy's *Dar Hazar* [*At Home*] (1987) is also a chronicle of the Islamic Revolution,[38] from the perspective, however, of a woman who is initially unsure about her feelings concerning revolution in general and eventually becomes certain of her dislike for the one underway. Those with whom she associates are not willing participants in the demonstrations. They are generally educated Iranians who have chosen, for the most part, a wait-and-see attitude.   Clearly resisting the anti-Western slogans of the revolution, Amirshahy avoids in *At Home* the negative references to the West that dominated the circles of the revolutionary groups. The Western characters that appear in her novel are neither presented as agents or symbols of Western imperialism nor with the sense of Otherness we have seen in many Iranian works of fiction. They are simply individuals who happen to be Westerners. In this respect, Amirshahy's own intimate familiarity with the West is undoubtedly an important factor.[39]   She avoids stereotypical portrayals of Western characters even in the few brief sketches she provides in her novel. This is not to say, however, that she intends to depict only the positive aspects of these characters. On the contrary, on several occasions in the novel, Western characters become the target of the biting satire for which Amirshahy is known. For example, when a BBC radio announcer refers to the shah without the normal ceremonial "His Majesty," the narrator satirically remarks that for this reason they are "seen as heroes by everyone."[40]   Later, her satiric subtlety turns against a newly arrived French woman, who, like many Western reporters dispatched to Iran at the time, suddenly becomes an expert on Iran. In a conversation with this French woman, the narrator reports:

> Claudine turns to me and says: "I have started my book."
> "I didn't know you were writing a book. What is it about?" I ask.
> "About the situation in Iran, that is, you might

say, the history of Iran, with the help of Jean
Jacques."
   "When you've just gotten off the plane!" I reply
laughing.
   Jean Jacques retorts: "What do you mean just off
the plane? Claudine has been in Iran for two
months already, right?"
   Claudine agrees.
   "And I have been here for some twenty days."
   I only raise my eyebrows in astonishment. Jean
Jacques either does not notice or interprets my
gesture as a sign of admiration, because he continues
to deliver the past and present half-truths and even
baseless rumors as decisively historical truths.[41]

In one of the few references Amirshahy makes to the anti-
American sentiments of the revolutionaries, her approach is once
again satirical. Reporting on the occupation and plunder of the
shah's palaces by the young revolutionaries, an eyewitness to the
events describes the following scene to the narrator:

Yes, today, they plundered all there was. ... When
they stormed in, an unfortunate crow had lost its
way and flown into the building through a broken
window. One of these revolutionaries who had a
gun began to shoot at the crow. When he was asked
why, he answered: This is the American Eagle; it
has to be destroyed![42]

The political symbolism, the anti-American and, on the
whole, anti-Western images during the Islamic Revolution in Iran
are powerful enough to influence the vision of writers who
would otherwise deal with apolitical aesthetics or merely social
concerns in their work. One such writer is Moniru Ravanipur,
in her experimental novel *Ahl-e Gharq* [*The Drowned*], which deals
with the brief history of a small, isolated community in southern
Iran.[43]   In terms of subject matter, style, and approach,
Ravanipur's novel did not conform to mainstream fiction writing
in the revolutionary and war-stricken climate of Iran at the time
of its publication. Perhaps for this reason, it attracted the
attention of readers and critics when it appeared in the winter
of 1989–1990, establishing her as a major post-revolutionary
fiction writer in the country.[44]

The locale, the characters, and the general atmosphere of *The Drowned* is reminiscent of Gholamhoseyn Sa'edi's *Fear and Trembling*, discussed in the previous chapter. Not unlike Sa'edi's story, *The Drowned* is the chronicle of the people of a small fishing village called Jofreh, on the Persian Gulf. Ravanipur devotes more than a hundred pages in the beginning of her novel to describing the traditional life and folklore of the handful of families who inhabit the small village. Without any contact or even awareness of the world outside their community, the people of Jofreh are content with their lives. The sea, to them, is both an endless source of sustenance and also a place of mystery, about which they hold certain superstitious beliefs. Busalmeh, for example, is the powerful ruler of the sea who occasionally becomes angry and takes away someone from their village, and they know that they must not do or say anything that might anger him. The sea protects the village from the outside world and allows the villagers to preserve their traditional life. But it is also the sea that brings them the first signs of imminent change. One day, the villagers find three boxes of colorful bottles filled with a fluid they have neither seen nor tasted before. Once the find is distributed among the inhabitants, according to the village custom, and they drink the contents of the bottles, the peace and tranquility of the village is disturbed for a few days. But the bottles are only the first sign of the impending intrusion of the outsiders into the lives of the villagers. Not long after, a small white boat appears on the sea and lands near the village. The initial reaction of the villagers to the boat is one of fear combined with curiosity. And when "three tall, blond men with blue eyes come out of the boat," the villagers wonder:

> Where in the world could these men of the sea have come from? It was not certain that they were human. ... Was Busalmeh playing a game on the drowned? Had he given them the power to reach land in the guise of others in order to drown the village? Or were they the dwellers of the sea coming to the village in human form?[45]

In their first visit, the "tall, blond men" give them more bottles of "magic drink" as well as some fruit. The village elder, who has seen the ill effects of the contents of the bottles on the people, is quite suspicious of the intent of the intruders, and many villagers break the bottles and decide that when the tall, blond men return, they will drive them out of the village. But some of the villagers have already developed a taste for the drink and secretly accept the gifts.

On subsequent visits, the intruders bring other gifts for the villagers, including some colorful plastic objects, for which the villagers have no use, and a "magic box" from which come voices that speak in strange tongues. For some time, until the batteries run out, the villagers neglect fishing and other chores, listening to the "magic box." Eventually, the tall, blond men return no more. However, with their visits and gifts, they have effected a permanent change in the lives of the villagers.

After these first visitors, other intruders find their way into this heretofore forgotten, remote village. A traveling salesman appears one day on a motorcycle, and at his instigation, gradually the villagers visit other villages and cities that they have now learned about. Political groups also learn about this village and coax the villagers to join them in demonstrations in the big city. The government has also discovered Jofreh, and with this discovery establishes a gendarmerie station and eventually decides to build a road to the village.

In a few years oil is discovered in Jofreh, and it soon becomes designated as a site for a vacation resort. The village elder, Zayer, sees the "world getting lost in the sound of small and large radios that men had brought from abroad."[46] People tell him about "blond women with blue eyes and about the oil wells that had appeared nearby."[47] Zayer, who represents the traditional life in Jofreh, is now "lost amidst the blond people in the city, the oil wells that had opened their mouths in villages far and near and the road building company that had ... set up business and was rapidly building a road to Jofreh."[48]

The Drowned is a novel that expresses a strong sense of nostalgia for the tranquility of traditional life. The arrival of Western intruders in the village marks the arrival of the modern age. To the villagers and to Ravanipur as well, all the outsiders that disturb and eventually destroy Jofreh, whether the "tall, blond men with blue eyes" or the Iranian government, are one and the same. The West brings modern industrial life into the village and so does the government with its modernization programs.

Towards the end of the novel, Ravanipur pays lip service to the revolution that finally removes the dictatorial hold of the gendarmes and government forces over the lives of the villagers, who have just recently been forced to get involved in the social and political world outside their village. But not even the revolution can prevent the complete destruction of whatever the Jofreh of the beginning of the novel represented, when at the end of the story the last inhabitant of the village "boarded up the doors and windows and, with hopes of returning to Jofreh some day, bought a small house in the city and migrated there."[49]

The clash between tradition and modernity is in one sense the clash between the Self and the Other. For many Iranians, the Self is defined in terms of tradition, but also in contrast to the Other. Modernity has been viewed by Iranians, particularly in this century, as a product of the West or the manifestation of Western culture which threatens Iranian traditional life and, therefore, the Iranian cultural identity, the Iranian collective Self. In the course of the Islamic Revolution in Iran, signs of a reaction to this threat were readily apparent in the anti-Western attitudes, the slogans and demonstrations that punctuated the upheaval. Blaming the West for imposing the dictatorial regime of the Pahlavis on the country and for all the problems and ills of the society would seem an inescapable reaction in the midst of the chaos and confusion that accompany any revolution. The initial reaction of many Iranian writers in such a climate and in keeping with the prevailing sentiments was just as simplistic. However, some writers from the very early days of the revolution began to reflect on the causes of the social problems more soberly than others and tried to seek the roots of these problems not simply in outside forces, in the actions of the Western or Westernized Other, but in the Iranian Self. In an interview conducted in the early months of the revolution, the notable writer and critic Hushang Golshiri, for instance, speaks of a "demon from within" that is at the root of the Iranian dilemma, a "demon" that exists within the Self of every individual, which can only be destroyed by that individual.[50]

Such contemplations of the Self and the struggles to find the roots of the dilemma in the Iranian Self and not in the Western Other are the subject of Esmail Fassih's (1983) *Sorayya dar Eghma* [translated as *Sorraya in a Coma*].[51] Fassih's novel is a story of contrasts. The narrator, Jalal Aryan, a Western-educated engineer who is deeply rooted emotionally and intellectually in the Iranian traditions, begins his journey from amidst the war-stricken chaos and confusion of the streets of Tehran to Paris, a world seemingly untouched, unaware, even oblivious to the one he has left behind. Scenes from the war, with the devastating effects of the bombings and the slaughter of innocent men, women, and children, flash through his mind as he sees before his very eyes the tranquil, peaceful life of the Parisians.

The purpose of Jalal Aryan's visit to Paris is to take charge of his niece, Sorraya, a young student in a deep coma as the result of a freak accident. But, the reader soon realizes, Fassih's purpose in this novel goes beyond relaying the story of a personal tragedy.

Sitting in an isolated spot on the shore of the River Seine, Jalal has been reading Frederick Forsyth's *Dogs of War*, a novel about the exploits of a group of international mercenaries in the "Republic of Zangaro," which has platinum mines worth millions of dollars. A British merchant with a small army of American, Irish, German, and French mercenaries has decided to overthrow the Zangaroan government and set up his own puppet state.[52] Fassih's narrator begins to see a parallel between the fate of the inhabitants of Zangaro in the story he is reading and his own as well as that of his country. The picture he paints of Zangaro (or Iran) is reminiscent of that by another fictional character, Ebrahim Beyg, in Maragheh'i's novel nearly a century earlier:[53]

> I have come here, in the middle of one of the most crucial upheavals ever to happen in the destiny of my people and my family. I am sitting in this corner, in this darkness, under this terrible rain, by this drunken river, next to this garbage dump, and cry in *Arabic*! Persian is of no use to me, and I do not know anything else. I am in Zangaroo [sic], and I am speaking Swahili. I am at the centre of a storm of reality, for which no language has yet been invented. And no one cares! Geographically, I am in Paris, in France. According to the Christian calendar, I am somewhere at the end of the 20th century. But I am in ancient Zangaroo [sic] ... In the era of "What the hell do we do now?" And in Zangaroo [sic], maps are drawn on the sands at the seashore, and history is written with dead men's saliva. In Zangaroo [sic], the calendars and clocks are numbered backwards. In Zangaroo [sic], after a change of regime, university professors are cab drivers, cab drivers are glassblowers, glassblowers are public prosecutors, public prosecutors are tobacco

planters, tobacco planters are policemen, policemen
are yoghurt-makers, yoghurt-makers are factory
engineers, factory engineers cook sheep's head and
feet, sheep's head and feet cooks are higher
education authorities, higher education authorities are
hubcap swipers, hubcap swipers are mat-weavers,
mat-weavers are spiritual leaders, spiritual leaders
are bulldozer drivers, bulldozer drivers are bean-
sellers, bean-sellers are senators, senators are dentists,
dentists are religious singers, religious singers are
pineapple distributors, pineapple distributors are
bookbinders, bookbinders are helicopter pilots, and
the pilots are all grave-diggers, because the grave-
diggers have fled to seek political asylum in [the]
neighboring country. In Zangaroo [sic], now babies
are born from the grave. Infants have hair and
beards, then they anti-grow, and enter the other life-
stages. After the years of youth, of power and
motion, they gradually forget how to walk, they
crumble and degenerate, and begin to crawl on all
fours. At the end of their life, they are placed in
their mother's womb, which is watered from the
sewers.[54]

Perhaps implicit in these reflections is the placing of blame
for the chaos described by the narrator on the Western powers.
The analogy between Zangaro with its platinum mines and Iran
with its oil reserves is obvious enough. But inherent in Fassih's
novel and in the passage just cited is the dilemma of Iranian
intellectuals, like the narrator, especially those who place the
blame for this chaotic situation on the West but who have left
Iran to live in Europe and America. On the one hand, on an
abstract level, the picture that they have formed in their minds
and presented in their work reflects the same image of the West
that their uneducated revolutionary compatriots projected in their
public demonstrations in the streets. On the other hand, on a
more concrete level, as the narrator of Fassih's novel discovers
in Paris, they admire and have fully succumbed to the West and
Western life, which has become an inseparable part of their Self.
The West that they had criticized, therefore, is an abstract
political West, and the one that they admire is the West of
technological and scientific advancement which affords them the
means of a comfortable, modern life. But this schizophrenic

portrayal of the West is not merely the product of the minds of Iranian intellectuals who have "chosen" a life of exile in the West, about whom a French character in the novel comments that they "start off a revolution and then run."[55]   Those who have not run away from the revolution are typified in the character of the young Iranian student studying in Paris toward a doctoral degree in chemistry who wants to take from the West, which he proclaims to despise and condemn, only its knowledge and technology.   In him, Fassih presents the approach of a post–Islamic Revolution Iran, which is trying to achieve what many writers of travel diaries advocated a century or more earlier.[56]

The predicament of the Westernized intellectuals explored by Fassih in *Sorraya in a Coma* is in fact that of an entire nation, a dilemma that Iranians have tried to resolve from their earliest contacts with the West in recent centuries.   The image or images of the West and Westerners in the Iranian psyche, as presented in fictional form, has in many ways reflected this quandary.   It is a complex predicament which is at the same time simple. Iranians have admired and envied Western progress and have suffered from a sense of inferiority when they have contrasted their own society with that of the West.   At the same time, whenever they have swallowed their pride, so to speak, and tried to learn from and emulate the West, they have found that in such a transaction they lose their traditional values and self identity.   In his novel, Fassih describes the Iranian intellectuals in exile as the "Lost Generation."   He is indeed describing all Iranians today who have lost their own traditional way of life without being able to fully absorb and be absorbed in what the West has offered them.   In his 1986 novel, *Dal* [Eagle], Mahmud Golabdarreh'i draws on the experiences of Iranians who have lived in exile in the West since the Islamic Revolution to explore this phenomenon.[57]

The protagonist of *Eagle* is Nabi, a writer-translator, who has decided after five years of living in Iran, separated from his family since the revolution, to join his wife and two daughters living in Sweden.   His wife and his daughters, one of grammar-school age and the other in her late teens, seem to have adjusted well to life in their new country.   His wife has found a job, and the children go to school.   They have all learned the new language and seem quite content in their new surroundings.   But their adjustment to Swedish life and values also means that they have changed such that Nabi feels he no longer recognizes them as members of his own family.

Nabi has reluctantly escaped a society which has moved on a course contrary to what he had envisioned as his own revolutionary ideals. But his escape to the West has brought him into a world that seems more alien and even more intolerable to him than the one which he has left behind. He sees an indication of the strong "otherness" of this world on his first night in Sweden. Sitting with his wife, like two strangers, in their small apartment he watches a program on television in which several people appear to be arguing. Since he does not understand the language, his wife explains:

> That man is a Turk. And that is his wife sitting next to him. His wife is Swedish. The man has two children. He has beaten one of his children. The government found out about it and took the child away from him. They asked the child about it, and he corroborated the charge. So, they took the second child away as well. The Turk has threatened that if they don't return his children to him, he will kill the children, his wife, and himself. Now, the Swedish government is in a dilemma as to what to do. There is a law that if a parent beats his or her child, the government will take the child away. But there is no law about returning the child. Now they have all gotten together and have been discussing what to do for a month. They want to convict the Turk and say to him: You have been in Sweden for fifteen years and are aware of and benefit from all Swedish laws. You benefit from insurance, vacation pay, and all the resources of the factory and other things. How is it that you did not know about this law and you beat your child? The Turk is becoming tame gradually and is giving in. At first, he only cursed and shouted. But now, look at him, sitting quietly not saying a word.[58]

To Nabi, who has just fled his own country because he did not want those in power to dictate to him how he or his children should dress or about his relations with his family, the Swedish system appears to be another kind of dictatorship. Sweden provides not only for its own citizens, but even for refugees, like Nabi and his family, such social services as

education, job training, and health care, free of charge. Refugees
like Nabi are even provided with living expenses for a period of
time while they attend language classes and become familiar
with the laws and customs of their new environment. But, as
Nabi gradually learns, there is a price to pay for all this. Other
incidents similar to the story of the Turk occur. An Iranian
friend of Nabi's is arrested for beating his wife. But instead of
being taken to jail, he is taken to a hospital where he is treated
for his "disorder." Some time later, on his way to the hospital
to bring the friend home, Nabi meets an acquaintance, an Iranian
engineer who has lived in Sweden for several years and is now
driving a bus. The bus driver's assessment of the Swedish social
system presents a "Brave New World" image of the West,
something that Nabi has been unable to articulate for himself.
The Iranian bus driver comments about the "hospital" and the
friend who was taken there:

> When someone is trapped there, it is for good. Even
> if they let him go, he will return like an addict, like
> a hand-trained pigeon, Mr. Nabi. That's the way
> they are themselves, and they want to make us
> become like them. If we fight and refuse to become
> like them, they tame us by force of pills and
> injections. They calm us down. They make us
> patient, compliant, meek and quiet. To tell you the
> truth, it's not just us; those who come to this society
> from other places must become like them after a
> while. If they don't, they cannot go on living. If
> they refuse it, they make them become like
> themselves with a thousand tricks, just like
> themselves.[59]

Like his friend, Nabi, too, eventually meets a similar fate.
After months of trying unsuccessfully to cope with Swedish life
and refusing to conform to values and laws he finds alien and
threatening to the vague notion of identity he is striving to
preserve for himself, in the heat of a domestic quarrel with his
wife, he breaks some pieces of furniture. His eldest daughter,
who, Nabi feels, has completely metamorphosed into a member
of this new society and is concerned about the destruction of the
property of "the poor, tax-paying Swedes," reports him to the
police. Nabi is subsequently taken away to a hospital and
placed under "treatment." His resistance to becoming a

conforming member of the society breaks down when he is given the injections his bus-driver friend had spoken of earlier: "When the fluid in the syringe began to flow into Nabi's veins, his sense of honor and pride, his complaining, moaning and groaning, protestation, and anger were eradicated from his veins, arteries, and roots."[60]

Golabdarreh'i this time chooses Nabi's Swedish doctor to confirm the picture presented earlier of Swedish society:

> I say, why did you want to escape through the
> window? If you wanted to go, you should have said
> so; we would have sent you on your way. We
> didn't ask you to come here. You came of your own
> accord. And now that you are here, why do you
> want to leave? If you want to, you can leave. But if
> you want to stay, if you want to stay here, you
> cannot be the Nabi that you were. This is not what
> I want. It is not what medical science and Swedish
> medical board want either. It is what you want. ...
> It does not matter where you were before and what
> was or is there. That does not concern us. You
> should have left the Nabi that you were, as you left
> the place that you left to come here. Did you not
> leave the place where you left? ... If you want to
> stay here, you must become our Nabi. You must
> become like us.[61]

The image of the Brave New World that Golabdarreh'i presents of Sweden extends to the West in general. The West appears as a great machine, a huge, powerful giant that wants to create, or rather recreate, the world in its own image.

In their encounter with this Western giant, Iranian writers in the post-revolutionary years have expressed a fear of being crushed politically, socially, and culturally. Their critical portrayal of the West represents their desperate effort, perhaps on behalf of their compatriots but also for themselves, to confront this indomitable adversary. But it is also an effort to understand the enemy, as it were, to comprehend the nature and character of the West. Ehsan Naraqi's pre-revolutionary observations about the West discussed at the beginning of this chapter are among such efforts from a socio-cultural perspective. In novels such as *The Mysteries of My Homeland* and *Cry for My Revolution, Iran*, Iranian authors present a very negative picture of the West and Westerners. But at the same time, in drawing their dark portrait, they are trying to explain and understand the Western giant politically. The simplicity, even superficiality, of the black and white imagery of the anti-Western revolutionary slogans also reflects such an attempt. Ravanipur's nostalgic glance at dying traditional life, Fassih's exploration of the state of Iranian identity, and Golabdarreh'i's story of one man's struggle to preserve his individuality are all reflections of reactions by these Iranian authors in their inevitable confrontation with the Brave New World, in their encounter with the West.

7

CONCLUSION: ON THE MIRROR AND THE IMAGE MAKERS

Specialists on Persian literature have argued that twentieth-century literature in Iran has had deeper roots in the Western literature of the recent centuries than in its own national heritage.[1] Although there is a tradition of storytelling in the form of long romances, for instance, both in prose and verse, the novel in its modern form is considered a genre imported from the West. Similarly, while shorter tales in the form of anecdotes have been a feature of classical Persian literature, the modern Persian short story is regarded essentially as an adopted literary form. In regard to drama, prior to the later decades of the nineteenth century, the only extant written documents are those verses which were used as scripts for the dramatic performances known as *ta'ziyeh*, or dramatizations of the martyrdom of various Shi'ite holy figures. Other dramatic performances consisted of satirical comedies or puppet shows which generally followed a common plot and were improvised by the players. The first modern, Western-style Persian plays were based on the works of European dramatists, and Iranian playwrights in the present century have kept at least one eye on the development of this art in the West.

Perhaps the most discernible signs of Western influence on Persian literature are witnessed with regard to Persian poetry. Aside from the changes in subject matter and poetic vision that marked New Poetry [*she'r-e no*], the most dramatic departure from classical verse occurred in form.[2] The work of the modernist poet is characterized in part by the importance placed on the unity and structure of a poem and the disregard for the essential formal features of classical poetry, namely meter and rhyme. A traditionalist poet or literary scholar, to whom such deviations from the classical convention were indefensible, could not and would not regard a "new poem" as a poem at all. In fact, the works of modernist poets were often dismissed as translations or blind imitations of Western poetry.

The argument evincing the rootedness of modernist Persian literature in the Western tradition is, of course, valid to some extent. Even though a rich cultural and literary heritage such as Persian has inevitably left its direct and indirect marks on the works of contemporary Iranian literary artists, the charge of a distinct Western influence on this literature can also be easily substantiated. For instance, Mohammad Ali Jamalzadeh, considered a pioneer in modern Persian fiction, wrote a manifesto of sorts in 1921 in which he argues for a change in Persian literature parallel with the changes in the society, pointing to Western literature as a model. He writes:

> Today, Iran is indeed behind most countries of the
> world on the road of literature. In other countries,
> literature has gradually gained variety, thereby
> capturing the soul of all classes of the nation,
> encouraged everyone, rich and poor, men and
> women, from grammar-school children to the elderly,
> to read and has brought spiritual progress for the
> members of those nations. In our country, Iran,
> however, generally deviation from the path of our
> ancestors is considered tantamount to the destruction
> of literature. On the whole, the same essence of
> Iranian political dictatorship which is known
> throughout the world can also be seen in its
> literature.[3]

Jamalzadeh then argues in support of following the contemporary Western path in literature and advocates fiction writing for the purpose of educating the masses:

> Upon first glance at the present literature of the
> West, one might conclude that because of the
> abundance of fiction, which today comprises a major
> portion of this literature, Western literature suffers
> from decadence and deficiencies, whereas without a
> doubt, at no time, nowhere in the world has
> literature advanced as it has at the present time in
> the West. A cursory glance at the life of the people
> of the West, where books have almost become
> necessary items of their lives, like forks and knives,

socks and handkerchiefs, is sufficient to prove this
point. And, of course, the main reason for this trend
is that writing now follows the path of the novel and
stories.[4]

Large numbers of translations from European and American
literatures during the present century and the interest that
literate Iranians have shown in the works of Western authors
point to the popularity of the notion verbalized by Jamalzadeh
in his 1921 remarks.[5] More important, however, are the changes
that took place in the overall attitude and approach of Iranian
writers in regard to content and form in their work. In terms
of content, influenced by the works of Western writers, Iranian
writers redirected their focus from the mystical themes and
panegyric and didactic verse that were the dominant forms of
traditional literary artists to the more mundane concerns of the
lives of the people and the world around them. The attention
that contemporary Western literature paid to ordinary members
of society and their depiction as main characters, particularly in
fiction and drama, also directly inspired the works of Iranian
writers who had been witnessing the social changes and the
populist movements in their own country since the latter part of
the nineteenth century. In aesthetic terms, new literary forms
that were often directly borrowed from or inspired by Western
literatures and which were introduced to Persian literature in the
first two decades of the present century have gradually
dominated the work of most literary artists in Iran. While it is
true that the traditional literary establishments and the
educational institutions have resisted, successfully for the most
part, the acceptance of modernist works as part of the Persian
literary cannon, it has also been true for many decades now that
the works of the modernists have captured the imagination of
younger educated Iranians and have dominated literary
production in Iran.[6]

The works that have been discussed in Chapters 3 through
6 of the present study are written in two genres, the novel and
the short story, which in their present forms developed in Iran
under Western influence. This, of course, is not to say that they
are by any means Western works written in Persian. The
influence of traditional Persian literature on modern fiction is
unquestionable, evident not only in works in which writers have
made a conscious effort to employ the form, style, and language
of traditional tales but in the totality of modern literature that

has developed in the particular Iranian cultural environment, as well. Nevertheless, the vehicle of expression is itself at least partly Western. It goes without saying, then, that the medium through which the images of the Western Other are reflected, as is examined in this study, should be familiar to the Western observer. By the same token, the traditional as well as the modernist Iranian literary artist is aware of the alien nature of this medium. Hence, while the traditionalist rejects the alien Western forms, the modernist struggles in the throes of the anxiety of Western influence and tries to justify his artistic endeavor. One outspoken modernist critic and writer, Reza Baraheni, observes:

> It is true that some manifestations in our culture in the present century have been strongly influenced by the West, indeed plagued by the West ..., but in the important cultural arenas, despite the copying of Western forms, our implementation has been authentic[ally Iranian] and in keeping with the necessities and requirements of our national culture. For instance, although Jamalzadeh took the form of fiction from the West, all the characters of the *Once upon a Time* collection [of short stories] and the utilization of language, expression and even the structure of the stories are strongly Iranian. Because we had been placed on the course of change in the general sense of the term, a man by the name of Jamalzadeh was conditioned by particular social and historical circumstances, and the result could be none other than *Once upon a Time*. The potential for the book existed; Jamalzadeh made that potential a reality.[7]

Such justification reveals the keen awareness on the part of the modernist of the tremendous influence of the West on his work. Baraheni further comments that Persian literature has been strongly influenced by the great Western works, either through translations of these works or the familiarity of Iranian writers with European languages and their reading of Western literature in the original. But in the same breath, he observes that the same Western literature that has influenced contemporary Iranian literature has been under the influence of Asian and African literatures since the Middle Ages. He writes:

> The form of Iranian lyric poetry [*ghazal*] has had a
> great influence on the Petrarchan sonnet and the
> English or Shakespearean sonnet. Prior to this
> influence, Dante had kept an eye both on the story of
> the Prophet's ascension to heaven [*me'raj*] from the
> Islamic point of view and the *Ardavirafnameh* [The
> Book of Ardaviraf] and on the whole on a
> combination of the Semitic and Iranian cultures.[8]

Leaving aside the fact that many readers may find questionable Baraheni's claim that Petrarch and Shakespeare were influenced by the *ghazal* in writing their sonnets, reactions and justifications by modernists of this sort have been primarily responses to the traditionalist Iranian literary establishment, which dismissed such literary innovators as Nima Yushij, the "father of New Poetry" in Iran, with the pejorative label of "Westernized." On the other hand, given the general anti-Western political leanings of the majority of the modernists, polemics of this kind function for them as a catharsis, a psychological self-exorcism of the Western evil spirit, if you will.

Yet, the traditionalists and those who have aligned themselves with the traditionalist literary camp, particularly in the academic institutions in Iran, have not been unaffected by Western influence. True, they have remained loyal to the classics and the classical conventions of Persian literature, but, paradoxically, they have also regarded Western Orientalist scholars with a certain degree of awe, often blindly accepting their contributions to Persian literary scholarship with the implicit understanding that since Westerners have gained superiority in other scientific fields, they must also be regarded as authorities in the field of Persian literature.[9] To the modernist, the traditionalist position is incongruous: on the one hand, the traditionalists condemn the "Westernization" of contemporary Persian literature, while on the other, they do not apply the same yardstick to Western influence over their own scholarship. In this respect, the dilemma of the traditionalist may not differ significantly from that of the modernist. The traditionalists' reaction to Western-style contemporary literature can be seen not only as an indication of their misplaced attempt to exorcise the alien Western spirit, but also in some ways as a boisterous castigation of the modernist brought on by subconscious guilt over having committed the sin of submitting to Western influence in their own scholarship and academic pursuits.

The schizophrenic stance of both modernist literary artists and traditionalist literary scholars is symptomatic of the shadow that Western literature and literary studies, and in general Western culture, have cast on Persian literature and Iranian culture. Various genres of modern Persian literature—the novel, the short story, new poetry, and drama—constitute an image of the West in and of themselves. In terms of form, the Western reader can readily recognize the Iran-ization of the Western literary genre, despite the fact that the writer may have also combined the borrowed Western forms with those that have existed indigenously in Iranian literature.[10] Moreover, a Persian short story or novel assumes the local coloring of its society and becomes Iranian. At first glance, the Western reader may find such works and the world they present strange and unfamiliar, a mirror that distorts his or her own images of the West, but upon closer scrutiny, through those same seemingly distorted images, the reader will recognize a likeness of the West. In his *Hedayat's "Blind Owl" as a Western Novel*, the study of an Iranian novel, Michael Beard offers the Western reader insight into Western literary tradition through a non-Western work. He presents to his Western reader an examination of *The Blind Owl* as "a commentary on its Western predecessors" and proposes using Hedayat's novel "as a lens through which to see, as if from outside, aspects of our own narrative fiction." He goes on to add that "the advantage is to help the Western reader ... to recognize ... when the alien under our scrutiny is in fact ourselves."[11]

For Iranian writers and perhaps many Iranians in general, the dilemma that they have faced in their encounter with the West is ontologically important to an understanding of themselves, their own place in today's world, and their relationship with other cultures, particularly the West. Their writings about the West and the images that they present of the West and Westerners, whether in fictional or non-fictional forms, function as a vehicle, an indication of their effort in this quest. For centuries, they have seen the West as an enigmatic apparition, both threatening and fascinating. Images of the Westerners that emerged from the Crusades characteristically presented a hostile Other to all Moslems, including the Iranians, whose encounters were more limited than those of other Moslems who fought in those wars. The occasional reflections of the *farangi*s in the works of poets such as Sa'di and Attar are therefore vague and always shaped by religious beliefs and attitudes, by the Moslem notions of the West as the abode of the hostile infidels.

In later centuries, with the relatively rapid scientific, technological, and social advancements in Europe and the increasing contact with Westerners, Iranians began to form in their own minds more defined images of the West and the Western Other. The enigma of the Western apparition, however, continued to persist. The influence of Western powers in the region and their pursuit of colonialist policies perpetuated the image of the hostile Other. At the same time, the advancements of the West in military and other technology made the West a source of envy for Iranians and created in them the desire to learn about Western sciences.

This dilemma of feeling simultaneously threatened and fascinated by the West developed into a sense of admiration and rejection of the West for Iranian travelers to Europe and America. They visited Western societies, encountered Westerners and interpreted what they had seen in the form of observations about the West in their travel diaries. The images of the West that are reflected in these mirrors are often selective and may not represent the totality of the object of scrutiny. They are piecemeal pictures that the writers place side-by-side to create a collage of the West, to reconstruct that object of scrutiny. The result is by definition subjective. The West in these works is a fiction that, like any fiction, has some basis in truth.

The travel diaries that dominated the Iranian literature of the nineteenth and early twentieth centuries reveal to us the attempt of Iranian visitors to the West to understand societies and peoples who were theretofore relatively unknown to them. Much of what they saw seemed to them a myriad of wonders and many of the customs and beliefs they encountered seemed strange, odd. But these visits and encounters also opened their eyes to wider horizons and they began to contrast Western progress with the stagnation of their own institutions. The West gradually transformed from being merely an object of wonder to a touchstone with which they could evaluate their own society and culture. Hence, the works of writers from the early to the middle decades of this century in which the West appears for the purpose of contrast often depict positive features of the West and reflect a Western image that is worthy of emulation.

But more than a land of wonders, an object of disinterested scrutiny, and a utopia, the West came increasingly to be regarded as a threat, politically and militarily, to Iranians who had espoused nationalist sentiments at least since the Constitutional Revolution in 1906 through the 1950s and the coming to power and eventual overthrow of the government of Dr. Mohammad Mosaddeq.   The Persian fiction of the post–World War II period mirrored initially anti-British and subsequently anti-American images.   The threat posed by the Western powers on the nationalistic sentiments of Iranians created a xenophobic impact.   It was a threat not only to the very foundations of Iranian political, but also cultural, identity. Stereotypical reflections of Westerners, therefore, became a feature of these stories by writers who, perhaps intentionally, presented the world in black and white, good and evil, and usually portrayed the Westerner negatively.

There is, of course, an underlying purpose on the part of a writer who presents one-dimensional images and stereotypical characters. With a story a writer, more than trying to provide the reader with an artistic representation of life, attempts to advance a cause, as it were, to rectify a wrong.   For a writer committed to social causes, literature becomes a vehicle through which to fight injustice.   The one-dimensional fictional characters and negative images of the West that appear in these works are often shallow and at best serve the momentary purpose for which they are intended.   But in the course of the development of the genres of the short story and the novel in Iran, these fictional creations also represented a phase that prepared Iranian writers to create more complex Western characters and multidimensional images of the West in the 1960s and 1970s.   A factor that must be taken into consideration in examining the images of the West and Westerners in the fiction of these decades is the significant exposure of Iranians to European and American societies and cultures.   Large numbers of Iranian students attended colleges and universities in Europe and the United States.   The number of Westerners living in Iran increased, particularly in large cities.   The expansion of the Iranian television networks brought American- and European-made programs about Western life to the homes of many Iranians who would otherwise have no immediate knowledge of the West and Westerners.   Hence, the West became less a place created in the imagination of Iranians and more an actual, tangible part of the world that they could readily visualize. Similarly, Iranians now began to see Westerners as "real" people and their languages, beliefs, and customs no longer as odd, but different.   In other words, the image of the strange Western Other gradually transformed into a more familiar one.   The Western Other was in some respects "humanized" for many Iranians. This process of familiarization is reflected in the works of writers of this period. Moreover, in these stories, while some blame is still placed on the West for the ills in Iranian society, because the West and Westerners are no longer seen as an all-encompassing evil, the Iranian literary artist delves deeper into the Iranian culture and collective psyche for the causes of those ills.

To some extent, with the onset of the Islamic Revolution in Iran, the clock in the development of Persian fiction in terms of the attitudes of writers toward their Western characters did not turn back.   With the fall of the Pahlavi regime, which was viewed by many Iranians as pro-Western and often identified as a common enemy along with the United States, writers begin to write more freely about the West, particularly in conjunction with the influence of Western power over the regime of Mohammad Reza Shah, without the fear of censorship. Negative images of the West openly appear alongside those of the overthrown Iranian regime.   Nevertheless, even when these writers create negative stereotypes of Westerners, their stereotyped and one-dimensional characters are much more complex and human than those in works of earlier fiction writers.   In other words, these fictional characters begin to assume some of the characteristics of the Iranian Self.   More importantly, in stories written in recent years, the West and Western characters often appear as incidental elements and components of the plot, without any particular attempt on the part of the writer to cast them either in a negative or positive light. In this vein, the writer and the Iranian protagonists of his or her stories seem much more interested in trying to understand the age-old dilemma of being both fascinated and threatened by the West, of accepting Western influence while espousing rejection of all things Western. In general terms, this dilemma is the same as that faced by Iranian travelers to the West since nearly two centuries ago. The difference between the attitude of the contemporary writers toward the West and that of their predecessors lies in the depth of their understanding of the West. The nineteenth century Iranian visitor to Europe viewed the West with suspicion and reconstructed for his readers an ambivalent picture of it. His understanding of Westerners was based on what he saw more or less as a detached observer, as a transient visitor to an exotic land whose journey would ultimately end.

The image that the contemporary writer presents of the West and Westerners is also ambivalent. Although more sophisticated in terms of his or her knowledge of the West, aware that the West cannot be ignored and dismissed as an imaginary entity, the land of infidels, the contemporary writer also approaches the West with suspicion.

In the contemporary writer's work, the image of the Western Other has become multidimensional and complex. But this multidimensionality and complexity of the image of the Other has also led to more in-depth contemplation of the Iranian Self. The question in regard to the West and Western influence for many writers up to the first half of the present century was essentially a sociological one. In contrast to the West, conditions in Iran were backward. The Iranian intellectual longed to select those features of the West that would bring about progress in his or her own society. In the past four decades, and even more so since the Islamic Revolution, the question has become a psychological, even a philosophical, one as Iranians have begun to define or redefine their Iranian Self vis-à-vis the non-Iranian, particularly Western, Other.

Images in the minds of the image makers are products of their perception of the object. But even though the image is born of perception, its impact on the masses and its manifestations in the society are often much greater and more powerful than those general perceptions of the populace. The sentiments of Iranian revolutionaries with regard to the United States in the 1978–1979 upheaval were clear enough to any observer. The power of the image of America as the Great Satan created by the leader of the uprising, Ayatollah Khomeini, however, helped articulate these sentiments in terms of the binary opposition of good and evil, and reinforced such sentiments in larger segments of the Iranian populace. In other words, while perceptions had previously contributed to the creation of the image, now the image itself contributed to the formation of the Iranian perception of America. Likewise, it can be argued that the images of the West and Westerners that appear in Persian fiction and which reflect the general Iranian sentiments and perceptions of the West can in turn have an impact on the formation of those perceptions. The extent of this impact, however, has been and will be by and large limited with regard to the general populace, given the relatively small number of readers of these works in Iran. These images, therefore, will have a greater impact on the intelligentsia in Iran, who have been the consumers of this literature.

But the influences of Iranian fiction in shaping perceptions about the West is an extraliterary question, one which should perhaps be of interest to sociologists. From a literary perspective, if Stendhal's metaphor for the novel can be extended to short stories as well, the Persian fiction we have examined in this study is a "mirror carried down the road" of Iranian cultural history, in which images of the West and Westerners are reflected.

Whether this mirror reflects the truth, whether the images are accurate reflections of the West or distortions of the object reflected in it, is a question, therefore, to which Iranians and Westerners, indeed any given individual, might give differing answers, responses which are necessarily subjective and based on each person's own viewpoint, cultural beliefs, and biases. In our "global village" of today, it would appear, neither nations nor individuals can survive within the confines of seclusion and isolation. Neither has the Iranian Self been able, for at least two centuries, to ignore the impact on and the relevance of the Western Other to his or her own life, nor, one might argue, can the West choose to dismiss the recent Iranian events as the inane reactions of an irrational Other. In the mirror of their fiction, Iranian literary artists have made an effort to understand and deal with the West, an introspective effort that implicitly reveals the reality of the impact of the West on their political, social, philosophical, economic, and cultural existence. This same mirror also reflects certain images of the West that are worthy of contemplation.

NOTES

1. Introduction

1. In an article published nearly two decades ago, Hafez F. Farmayan, in "Observations on Sources for the Study of Nineteenth- and Twentieth-Century Iranian History," *International Journal of Middle East Studies* 5 (January 1974):33, writing on the clash between tradition and modernity and the inevitable seeming victory of the latter, remarks: "A tremendous sense of guilt haunts Iranian society for having profited in the abandonment of its tradition and ... this is the reason for the present misadjustment of the Iranian people to their new Westernized ideals and aims."

2. For instance, Khaqani, the twelfth-century poet, uses the term *farang* in the following lines: "I find your dog-keeper to be the king of *farang* / I see your doorman to be the king of Asqalan." Other occasional uses of the terms also exist in classical verse to describe certain objects from the West, such as Sa'di's *der'-e farangi* [Western armor] and the fifth-century poet Jami's *shisheh-ye farang* [literally European glass, i.e., eyeglasses].

3. *Morals Pointed and Tales Adorned: The "Bustan" of Sa'di*, trans. G. M. Wickens (Leiden: E. J. Brill, 1974), p. 188. Also see the original: Sa'di, *Bustan*, ed. Nurollah Iranparast, 2d ed. (Tehran: Danesh, 1976), p. 293.

4. Sa'di, *Gulistan or Flower Garden*, trans. James Ross (London: Walter Scott, Ltd., 1823), pp. 150–151.

5. Sheykh Faridoddin Mohammad Attar-Neyshaburi, *Manteq ot-Teyr*, 4th ed., ed. Seyyed Sadeq Gowharin. The story discussed appears as "Hekayat-e Sheykh Sam'an [San'an]," pp. 67–88. The most recent translation of this work is *The Conference of the Birds*, trans. Afkham Darbandi and Dick Davis.

6. For an elaboration on the concepts of *dar al-Eslam* and *dar al-harb*, see, for example, Frederick Mathewson Denny, *An Introduction to Islam*, p. 352.

7. For a general and insightful historical look at Iranian perceptions of the West, see Roger Savory, "Muslim Perceptions of the West: Iran" in *As Others See Us: Mutual Perceptions, East and West*, ed. Bernard Lewis, Edmund Leites, and Margaret Case, in *Comparative*

Civilizations Review 13 (Fall 1985) and 14 (Spring 1986):73–89.

8. James Morier, *The Adventures of Hajji Baba of Ispahan*, ed. C. J. Wills.

9. Ibid., pp. 544–546.

10. As we shall see in the discussion on travel diaries in the following chapter, an increasing number of Iranians traveled to Europe and America in the nineteenth century. Iranian kings, such as Naseroddin Shah Qajar and later Mozaffaroddin Shah Qajar, as well as other dignitaries were among such travelers. Sending students to learn about the West and Western progress also began during the nineteenth century. By the turn of the century, stories told by earlier visitors to the West had encouraged people from various walks of life, including businessmen, to travel to the West.

11. For an account of the Western governments' involvement in these events, see Kermit Roosevelt, *Countercoup: The Struggle for the Control of Iran*.

12. On Reza Shah's modernization efforts, see Amin Banani, *The Modernization of Iran (1921–1941)*.

13. For an interesting account of the impact of Reza Shah's actions to force women to remove their veils, see a story by Jalal Al-e Ahmad, "Jashn-e Farkhondeh" [Joyous Celebration] in *Panj Dastan*, 4th ed.

2. Understanding the Unknown

1. This is the "Orient" that Edward Said describes in his *Orientalism*.

2. Homa Nateq, "Farang va Farangma'abi va Resaleh-ye Enteqadi-ye Sheykh va Shoyukh," *Zaman-e No* 12 (1986):49.

3. Naser Khosrow Qobadiyani-Marvazi, *Safarnameh-ye Naser Khosrow*, 2d ed., ed. Nader Vazinpur.

4. A similar genre, called *sefaratnameh*, was popular in other countries, especially in the Ottoman Empire. The *sefaratnameh*, or "embassy account," was perhaps more official than the *safarnameh*. For a study of this genre, see Fatma Müge Göçek, *East Encounters West: France and the Ottoman Empire in the Eighteenth Century*.

5. Mirza Abu Taleb Khan, *Masir-e Talebi ya Safarnameh-ye Mirza Abu Taleb Khan*, 2d ed., ed. Hoseyn Khadiv-Jam.

6. Ibid., p. 80. His preference for the Irish over the English may be partially biased, the result of his blaming the English officials in India who had provoked him to kill the rajah but had failed to keep their promises to support him.

7. Ibid., p. 81. He also observes that the "Irish live in moderation. Neither like the English do they live with pomp and circumstance nor like the Scots do they strive to gain wealth and position."

8. Ibid., p. 80.

9. Ibid.

10. This is true of virtually all the early Iranian travelers to the West. Even as late as the last decade of the nineteenth century, members of other classes were only occasionally represented among the visitors to the West.

11. Abu Taleb, p. 231.

12. Ibid. Given his status as a dignitary in India, Mirza Abu Taleb would have considered it beneath him to shop, a task which was relegated to servants.

13. Ibid.

14. Ibid. With regard to those who violate the laws, he writes further on that "if judges delay the case two or three days for consultation, the people begin to curse and insult them, because the people feel hostile towards him [the violator] for three reasons: firstly, for having committed the act; secondly, because they are ashamed of being a compatriot of his; and, thirdly, because his action will cause the simple and negligent people to follow his example and break the laws, which indeed causes everyone's contempt" (p. 231).

15. Ibid., p. 232.

16. Ibid., p. 225.

17. Ibid., p. 226. Although in his comparison of English and Moslem rules and means of "controlling" women he favors the former, his preference and general understanding of how women should be treated reveal not only such practices in the British society of his time, as he saw them, but also his own attitude toward them. About the British, he writes: "Their laws permit that a husband, should his wife act contrary to his wishes, may imprison her in a room for some time and may beat her with a stick that would not break her limbs. Hence, [women] would not even dare to engage in verbal arguments and in causing minor problems."

18. Ibid.

19. Ibid., p. 270.

20. Ibid., p. 306.

21. Ibid., p. xxvi, according to Iraj Afshar in the introduction to this travel diary.

22. Mirza Saleh Shirazi (Kazeruni), *Gozaresh-e Safar*, ed. Homayun Shahidi. Mirza Saleh arrived in England only two years after the end of the Russo-Iranian wars that began in 1804 and continued to 1813, resulting in the defeat of Iran and the signing of the Golestan Treaty of 1813, by which Russia gained control over the Caucasian territories. In the wake of this defeat as well as certain treaties signed between Iran and England, a group of students, including Mirza Saleh, were sent to England on the initiative of Abbas Mirza, the Crown Prince, and the grand vizier, Qa'em Maqam Farahani, to learn military and other sciences. For more information, see the introduction to the volume under discussion. In English, see, Nikki R. Keddie, *Roots of Revolution: An Interpretive History of Modern Iran*, pp. 40–44.

23. Ibid., p. 205.

24. The first newspaper in Iran, called *Kaghaz-e Akhbar*, was published in 1836.

25. Hasan Morsalvand, ed., *Heyratnameh: Safarnameh-ye Abolhasan Khan Ilchi beh Landan*.

26. Ibid., p. 308.

27. Ibid., p. 181.

28. Ibid., p. 221.

29. In fact, his apparently graphic descriptions of his encounters with various women in England were offensive enough to the editor of the volume to cause him to omit passages, even pages,

in several instances (e.g., pp. 83, 104, 110, 120, 144, 199).

30. Hoseyn ebn-e Abdollah Sarabi, *Makhzan ol-Vaqaye': Safarnameh-ye Farrokh Khan Aminoddowleh*, ed. Karim Esfahanian and Qodratollah Rowshani.

31. Aminoddowleh was sent to Europe as an envoy of the Iranian government in 1856. This visit resulted in the signing of a well-known treaty with England on March 4, 1857, according to which Iran relinquished its claim on Herat.

32. Although one can assume that the scribe writes a chronicle of what seems important to himself—after all, he is the one in control of pen and paper—the content of the diary is, of course, dictated for the most part by the places and people the ambassador visits and by the fact that the final record would undoubtedly have had to receive the ambassador's approval.

33. Sarabi, p. 184.

34. Ibid., p. 276.

35. Ibid., p. 272.

36. Ibid., p. 372.

37. Ibid., p. 375.

38. The French king referred to is Napoleon III.

39. Sarabi, p. 270.

40. Ali Dehbashi, ed., *Safarnameh-ye Haj Sayyah beh Farang*.

41. Ibid., p. 102. These, however, are Sayyah's private thoughts, which he does not express openly to the Europeans with whom he comes in contact. Elsewhere in the diary, he recounts a visit to a learned European who asks him to interpret an Arabic verse. He does so, but adds that he is not a learned man by the standards of his own country. When the European scholar retorts, how was it that he could interpret the poem and comment on his knowledge of Turkish and French, Sayyah simply responds, "In my country, most people know six or seven languages" (pp. 224–225).

42. Ibid., p. 200.

43. Ibid., p. 226.

44. No information is extant on his impressions of his previous travels.

45. Hafez F. Farmayan, ed., *Safarnameh-ye Haji Pirzadeh*, vol. 1, 2d ed., *Az Tehran ta Landan*, p. 192.

46. Ibid., p. 248.

47. Ibid., pp. 252–253.

48. Ibid., p. 278. Pirzadeh adds in regard to those who try to commit suicide because of destitution that there are guards watching the rivers to rescue them. His bittersweet description condemns the social condition of Europe at that time which leaves no alternative for the poor but suicide, but also praises the Europeans for their conscientious efforts to prevent it.

49. Ibid., p. 238.

50. Ibid., pp. 247–248.

51. Ibid., p. 249.

52. Ibid. For a discussion of this work and a translation of this passage, see Roger Savory, "Muslim Perceptions of the West: Iran," in *As Others See Us: Mutual Perceptions, East and West*, ed. Bernard Lewis, Edmund Leites, and Margaret Case, in *Comparative Civilizations Review* 13 (Fall 1985) and 14 (Spring 1986):73–89.

53. Ibid. Interestingly, similar observations have been made since Pirzadeh, including those made following the Islamic Revolution, with regard to Iranian students both in Iran and abroad who have assumed various aspects of Western dress and behavior.

54. Ibid., p. 263.

55. Ibid., p. 286. A translation of this passage also appears in Savory, "Muslim Perceptions of the West," p. 85.

56. Quoted by Iraj Afshar in "Bahsi dar Asnad-e Marbut beh Farrokh Khan" in the introduction to Sarabi, *Makhzan ol-Vaqaye'*, p. 26.

57. Homayun Shahidi, ed., *Safarnameh-ye Shikago: Khaterat-e Haj Mirza Mohammad Ali Mo'inossaltaneh beh Orupa va Amrika.*

58. Ibid., p. 295.

59. Ibid., p. 299.

60. Ibid., p. 295.

61. Ibid., p. 443.

62. Ibid., pp. 472–473. Mo'inossaltaneh's description of his travel experiences in Europe on his return from America is recorded in a summary fashion. Generally, he merely notes days, dates, and names of cities he visited or hotels in which he stayed. His comments in passing may be partly due to the fact that the novelty of Europe had by this time worn off.

63. Mohammad Moshiri, ed., *Safarnameh-ye Ebrahim Sahhafbashi-Tehrani*, pp. 28–29.

64. Ibid., p. 48. Sahhafbashi's tongue-in-cheek suggestion to Iranians wishing to see the West seems to have been taken up in the early decades of the following century. A popular form of entertainment found in Iran as late as the 1950s was "Shahr-e Farang," literally "European City," a nickelodeon-type apparatus carried by vendors which would for a small fee show, among other things, pictures of European cities through a magnifying glass.

65. Ibid., p. 35.

66. Ibid., p. 37.

67. Ibid., p. 79. This comment concerns Canadians in the city of Victoria, British Columbia. On the whole, however, Sahhafbashi's views apply to the people of the United States as well. There is a note of praise in the author's description of small children who are raised to be independent and learn to be industrious and earn money in such jobs as shining shoes, selling newspapers, and acting as guides to visitors to the cities (p. 78).

68. Iranian travel diaries written in the middle decades of the twentieth century include Mohammad Ali Eslami-Nodushan, *Azadi-ye Mojassameh: Darbareh-ye Eyalat-e Mottahedeh-ye Amrika* [Liberty of the Statue: On the United States of America], and Mohammad Ebrahim Bastani-Parizi, *Az Pariz ta Paris: Haft Shahr, Haft Jush, Haft Rang* [From Pariz to Paris: Seven Cities, Seven-Metal Alloy, Seven Colors].

69. Interest in the military discipline and organization of the West by Iranian travelers to Europe in the nineteenth century had an important impact in the early decades of the twentieth century. Reza Shah Pahlavi's reign (1925–1941) was, for instance, characterized by his creation of an orderly

military and the imposition of discipline over the entire society. Emulation of these aspects of the West were manifested not only in the military, but even in the uniformity of dress of elementary school children.

70. Many aspects of European and Western societies in general fascinated Iranian reformists and rulers, resulting at times in superficial imitation of the West. In many respects, both Pahlavi monarchs tried to change the appearance of parts of Tehran, for instance, to resemble a Western city. In his feature film *Kalagh* [Crow] (1976), Bahram Beyza'i, the renowned writer and movie director, uses the nostalgic reminiscences of a character to recreate a 1930s street scene in Tehran which shows the government attempt at this kind of Westernization.

71. See, for example, Farmayan, *Safarnameh-ye Haji Pirzadeh*, pp. 247–248, 285–286; Shahidi, *Safarnameh-ye Shikago*, pp. 123–126; and Moshiri, *Safarnameh-ye Sahhafbashi*, pp. 54–56.

72. Comments of this nature are found, for instance, in Shahidi, *Safarnameh-ye Shikago*, and Moshiri, *Safarnameh-ye Sahhafbashi*.

73. An example is found in Shahidi, *Safarnameh-ye Shikago*, p. 228.

74. One such example is *Makhzan ol-Vaqaye'*, the travel diary of an important official, Farrokh Khan Aminoddowleh, which was actually written by Hoseyn ebn-e Abdollah Sarabi (see Note 30 for this chapter).

3. The West in Contrast

1. On the Iranian Constitutional Revolution, see E. G. Browne, *The Persian Revolution of 1905-1909*.

2. Zeynol'abedin Maragheh'i, *Siyahatnameh-ye Ebrahim Beyg*. This is in fact a three-volume work, with the first volume having had the greatest impact in Iran at the time. For a discussion of this work, see Hassan Kamshad, *Modern Persian Prose Literature*, pp. 17–21.

3. Ibid., p. 9.

4. Ibid., pp. 219–220.

5. Ibid., p. 5.

6. Ibid., p. 44.

7. Ibid., p. 117. Qazvin is located in northeast Iran and was the capital of the Safavid dynasty (1502–1736) before Shah Abbas chose Esfahan to replace it.

8. Ibid., p. 178.

9. Mohammad Ali Jamalzadeh, "Bileh Dig Bileh Choghondar" in *Yeki Bud, Yeki Nabud*. This collection has been translated by Heshmat Moayyad and Paul Sprachman as *Once upon a Time*. The story also appears in *Stories from Iran: A Chicago Anthology, 1921-1991*, ed. Heshmat Moayyad, pp. 33–46.

10. In this and other stories of *Once upon a Time*, Jamalzadeh criticizes not only the rulers but also the clerics. Because of Jamalzadeh's criticism of the latter in particular, the book stirred up a great deal of emotion upon its publication and copies of the book were burned on the streets. See also Kamshad, p. 94, and the introduction to the Moayyad and Sprachman translation cited above.

11. Jamalzadeh, *Once upon a*

Time, p. 96.

12. Ibid., p. 97.

13. Ibid., p. 98.

14. Ibid., p. 97.

15. On this point, see Reza Baraheni, *Qessehnevisi*, 2d ed., pp. 522–535; and Ahmad Karimi-Hakkak, in his review of a translation of Jamalzadeh's *Isfahan Is Half the World* in *Iranian Studies* 18 (Spring–Autumn 1985):423–424.

16. Sadeq Hedayat, *Karvan-e Eslam: Al-Be'sat ol-Eslamiyyah Ela al-Belad al-Faranjiyyah*, 2d ed.

17. Ibid., pp. 12-13.

18. Ibid., p. 13.

19. See Chapter 1 for a brief description of "the abode of war."

20. Hedayat, p. 19.

21. Ibid.

22. Ibid., p. 40.

23. On Hedayat's anti-Islamic beliefs, see Kamshad, pp. 137–201.

24. Hedayat, p. 40.

25. Such notions are expressed implicitly and explicitly in much of twentieth-century Iranian fiction.

26. Sadeq Hedayat, *Tup-e Morvari* (Tehran: Sazman-e Jonbesh-e Nasiyunalisti-ye Daneshgahiyan va Daneshpezhuhan va Rowshanbinan-e Iran, 1980). Two other editions also exist, including *Tup-e Morvari*, ed. Iraj Bashiri. This book has been continually banned in Iran.

27. Sadeq Hedayat, "Takht-e Abu Nasr" in *Sag-e Velgard*, pp. 75-100.

28. Hedayat apparently had more than a passing interest in ancient Iranian rites and witchcraft. See Kamshad, p. 188, and also Hedayat's article in French, "Le Magic en Perse," reprinted in *Neveshtehha-ye Parakandeh*, pp. 625–640.

29. Sadeq Hedayat, "S.G.L.L." in *Sayeh Rowshan*, 5th ed., p. 10.

30. Sadeq Hedayat, "Havasbaz" in *Parvin Dokhtar-e Sasan*, 3d ed., pp. 149–168 (the same story appears as "Lunatique" in French in the same collection); "Ayeneh-ye Shekasteh" in *Seh Qatreh Khun*, 8th ed., pp. 88–101; and "Katya" in *Sag-e Velgard*, pp. 63–74; *Buf-e Kur*, 14th ed. For a translation of this novel, see *The Blind Owl*, trans. D. P. Costello. Some two dozen of Hedayat's stories have been translated into English, published in *Sadeq Hedayat: An Anthology*, ed. Ehsan Yarshater, and *"The Blind Owl" and Other Hedayat Stories*, comp. Carol L. Sayers and ed. Russell P. Christensen.

31. Hedayat committed suicide in Paris in 1951. Many critics have commented on reflections of his own character and personality in his work. He became a sort of personality cult figure for many young Iranians and fiction writers.

32. Hedayat, "Sag-e Velgard" in *Sag-e Velgard*, pp. 9–21.

33. This quotation is taken from the translation of this story by Brian Spooner, "The Stray Dog," in Ehsan Yarshater, ed., *Sadeq Hedayat: An Anthology*, p. 121.

34. Kamshad, p. 185.

35. Mohammad Hejazi, *Sereshk*, p. 2.

36. Ibid.

37. Hejazi received the first Royal Prize for *Tears* and another novel entitled *Parvaneh*. See Kamshad, p. 77.

38. American television "soap operas" became very popular in Iran in the late 1960s and 1970s

and were shown regularly at prime time.

39. The Russian critic is D. S. Komissorov, quoted in Kamshad, p. 79.

40. The novel was published immediately after the fall of Prime Minister Mohammad Mosaddeq and the chaos of factional civil unrest in Iran.

41. See, Kamshad, p. 74, and also Hasan Abedini, *Sad Sal Dastannevisi dar Iran*, vol. 1, 2d ed., *1253–1342 [1874–1963]*, p. 79, who considers the establishment of this agency to have been for the purpose of "supervision, censorship, and controlling minds."

42. Hadi Hasan, trans. *A Golden Treasury of Persian Poetry*, p. 226.

43. On this event, see R. K. Ramazani, *The United States and Iran: The Patterns of Influence*, pp. 7, 14, and also Nikki R. Keddie, *Roots of Revolution: An Interpretive History of Modern Iran*, p. 77.

44. Hasan, trans., pp. 210–211.

45. Mohammad Mas'ud, *Golha'i keh dar Jahannam Miruyad*.

46. Ibid., pp. 28–29.

47. Ibid.

48. Ibid., p. 5.

49. Ibid., p. 17.

50. Ibid., pp. 103–104.

51. Ibid., p. 102.

52. This should, of course, be viewed in the context of the anti-Islamic sentiments that had developed in Iran since the late nineteenth century.

53. Mas'ud, pp. 124–125.

4. The Xenophobic Impact

1. Iraj Pezeshkzad, *Da'ijan Napel'on*, 12th ed.

2. Ibid., pp. 354–364.

3. Ibid., publisher's preface.

4. Pezeshkzad's novel was made into a very successful television serial in Iran by the well-known film maker, Naser Taqva'i, prior to the Islamic Revolution. The popularity of the serial was due in part to Iranian audiences recognizing in the character of Uncle Napoleon traits of their own relatives and acquaintances of his generation.

5. On Anglo-Iranian relations, see Abdolreza Hushang Mahdavi, *Tarikh-e Ravabet-e Khareji-ye Iran az Ebteda-ye Dowran-e Safavi-ye ta Payan-e Jang-e Jahani-ye Dovvom* [The History of Iranian Foreign Relations from the Beginning of the Safavid Period to the End of World War II], 3d ed.

6. See, for instance, Firuz Kazemzadeh, *Russia and Britain in Persia, 1864–1914*.

7. Mohammad Hoseyn Roknzadeh-Adamiyyat *Daliran-e Tangestani*, 7th ed. (Tehran: Entesharat-e Eqbal, 1975).

8. Ra'is Ali Tangestani became a folk hero and a symbol of anti-British resistance. The protagonist of Sadeq Chubak's 1963 novel, *Tangsir*, 2d ed. (Tehran: Javidan, 1968), himself a sort of folk hero, boasts of having fought the British under Ra'is Ali's command.

9. Roknzadeh-Adamiyyat, p. 108.

10. Simin Daneshvar, *Savushun*, 9th ed. For a translation, see *Savushun: A Novel About Iran*, trans. M. R. Ghanoonparvar. All subsequent references to this novel are from this translation.

11. Ibid, p. 21.

12. Ibid.

13. Ibid.

14. Ibid., p. 195.

15. Ibid., p. 32.

16. Ibid., p. 169.

17. Ibid., p. 132.

18. Ibid., p. 166.

19. Ibid., p. 32.

20. Ibid., p. 177.

21. Ibid., p. 30.

22. Naser Hariri, *Honar va Adabiyyat-e Emruz*, p. 33.

23. Ahmad Mahmud, *Hamsayehha*, 4th ed.

24. Ibid., p. 80.

25. Ibid., p. 88.

26. Ibid., p. 90.

27. Ibid., p. 134.

28. Ibid., p. 135.

29. Ibid., p. 212.

30. Asghar Elahi, "Ruz-e Nahs" in *Dastanha-ye No*, ed. Jamal Mirsadeqi.

31. Ibid., pp. 148–149.

32. For an account of these events, see Kermit Roosevelt, *Countercoup: The Struggle for the Control of Iran*. In the first edition of this book, the author implicated both British and American intelligence agencies in orchestrating the anti-Mosaddeq coup d'etat, which resulted in a recall of that edition under pressure from British authorities. At least two translations into Persian of this work were made immediately after the publication of this first edition, and one translation was serialized in a London-based Persian-language newspaper.

33. Translations of this work include, Jalal Al-e Ahmad, *Plagued by the West (Gharbzadegi)*, trans. Paul Sprachman, and *Gharbzadegi (Weststruckness)*, trans. John Green and Ahmad Alizadeh.

34. Al-e Ahmad, *Plagued*, trans. Sprachman, p. 4.

35. Al-e Ahmad, *Gharbzadegi*, trans. Green and Alizadeh, p. 13.

36. Al-e Ahmad, *Plagued*, trans. Sprachman, p. 4.

37. Ibid., p. 5.

38. This is true even of his allegorical stories, such as *Sargozasht-e Kanduha* [The Story of the Beehives] and *Nun val-Qalam* [By the Pen]. Even though the former story has a swarm of bees for its characters and the latter story is set in some fictional medieval time, they both deal with specific and general contemporary social and political issues.

39. Jalal Al-e Ahmad, *Modir-e Madreseh*, 7th ed.

40. Jalal Al-e Ahmad, *The School Principal*, trans. John K. Newton, p. 84.

41. Ibid., p. 88.

42. Jalal Al-e Ahmad, "Showhar-e Amrika'i" in *Panj Dastan* [Five Stories], 4th ed.

43. Ibid., p. 69. A translation of this story by Judith Wilks appears in Heshmat Moayyad, ed., *Stories from Iran: A Chicago Anthology, 1921-1991*, pp. 153-167; however, the translations of passages from this story are my own.

44. Ibid.

45. Ibid., p. 75. Also see Simin Daneshvar's interview (Al-e Ahmad was married to Daneshvar) in Hariri, p. 32.

46. Al-e Ahmad, "Showhar-e Amrika'i," p. 76.

47. Ibid., p. 79.

48. Ibid., p. 80.

49. Jalal Al-e Ahmad, *Sargozasht-e Kanduha*, 5th ed.

50. Hasan Abedini, *Sad Sal Dastannevisi dar Iran*, vol. 1, 2d ed., 1253–1342 [1874-1963, p. 208.

51. Gholamhoseyn Sa'edi, *Dandil*, 3d ed.

52. Sa'edi, "Dandil," trans. Hasan Javadi, in *Dandil: Stories from Iranian Life*, trans. Robert Campbell, Hasan Javadi, and Julie S. Meisami, p. 18.

53. Ibid., p. 24.

54. Ibid., p. 25.

55. Ibid., p. 28.

5. Split Images

1. This work appears in three volumes. Hoseyn Madani, *Esmal dar Niyuyork*, vol. 1, 4th ed.; vol. 2, 2d ed.; and vol. 3, 2d ed.

2. The term *jahel* literally means "ignorant," but commonly refers to *lut* or *lat*, members of an urban social group with chivalrous but simultaneously bandit-style characteristics. For some background information, see William F. Floor, "The Political Role of the Lutis," in *Modern Iran: The Dialectics of Change and Continuity*, eds. Michael Bonine and Nikki Keddie, p. 86; and Hamid Naficy, "Iranian Writers, the Iranian Cinema, and the Case of *Dash Akol*," *Iranian Studies* 18, nos. 2–4 (Spring–Autumn 1985):231–251.

3. Many of the situations in this novel seem contrived, sometimes for the sake of humor, and often to show the differences between the two cultures. It is, for instance, never explained how Esmal, who has had to work on a ship for his fare to the United States, could afford to stay for weeks in a luxurious hotel such as the Waldorf. Also, language does not seem to create problems for Esmal, who can at times converse comfortably with Americans but at

other times needs the assistance of William as an interpreter.

4. Madani, vol. 1, p. 89.

5. Madani, vol. 3, p. 94.

6. The *jahel* would usually consider it his duty to protect and fight for a woman's honor.

7. Madani, vol. 1, p. 100.

8. Ibid., p. 59.

9. Ibid.

10. Madani, vol. 2, p. 11.

11. Ibid., p. 15.

12. Madani, vol. 3, p. 152.

13. Madani, vol. 1, p. 80.

14. Naser Taqva'i, "Aqa Julu," *Arash* 2, no. 1 (Summer 1964): 84–94.

15. For a translation of this story, see "Agha Julu," in Minoo S. Southgate, ed. and trans., *Modern Persian Short Stories*, pp. 89–103.

16. Gholamhoseyn Sa'edi, *Tars va Larz*, 6th ed.

17. Gholamhossein Sa'edi, *Fear and Trembling*, trans. Minoo Southgate, pp. 119–120.

18. See comments by Minoo Southgate in her introduction to the translation of this collection, p. xxii. She observes that this episode of *Fear and Trembling* reflects the material prosperity of the final years of the shah's reign, "when huge increases in the oil revenues brought riches and prosperity to many Iranians," but also when "to share in the oil wealth, foreign businessmen, advisors, technicians, contractors and companies went to Iran."

19. Khosrow Shahani, "Borj-e Tarikhi" in *Vahshatabad* [City of Horror], 4th ed.

20. For an English translation of this story, see Southgate, ed. and trans., *Modern Persian Short Stories*, pp. 173–179.

21. Simin Daneshvar, "Eyd-e Iraniha," in *Shahri Chun Behesht*, 2d ed.

22. This kind of U.S. aid was provided through a program referred to as Point Four, and other such programs.

23. For an analysis of this story, see M. R. Ghanoonparvar, "Ba Neqab-e Siyah: Tahlili az Seh Dastan-e Kutah-e Simin Daneshvar," *Nimeye-Digar* 8 (Fall 1988):165–179.

24. Sadeq Chubak, "Asb-e Chubi," in *Cheragh-e Akhar*. For a translation of this story by John R. Perry, see *Stories from Iran: A Chicago Anthology, 1921-1991*, edited by Heshmat Moayyad, pp. 99–110.

25. For a more detailed discussion of this aspect of Chubak's work, see M. R. Ghanoonparvar's introduction to the translation of Sadeq Chubak, *The Patient Stone*, pp. ix–xxiv; M. R. Ghanoonparvar, *Prophets of Doom: Literature as a Socio-Political Phenomenon in Modern Iran*, pp. 80–83; and also, Reza Baraheni, *Qessehnevisi*, 2d ed., pp. 539–558.

26. Hushang Golshiri, *Jobbeh-khaneh*. "The Antique Chamber" is the title story of this volume. The writer prefers the term novel or novella with reference to this story. *Keristin va Kid*, 2d ed.

27. Golshiri, "Jobbehkhaneh," p. 23.

28. Ibid., p. 63.

29. Ibid., p. 69.

30. Ibid., p. 71.

31. Ibid. According to the author in his introduction to this volume of short stories, the published story is a revised version in which he was "able to say what could not be said [before], since this was a time for frankness" (p. 5).

32. Hushang Golshiri, *Shazdeh Ehtejab*, 7th ed., which appears in English translation as *Prince Ehtejab*, Minoo R. Buffington, trans., in *Literature East and West* 20 (1976):250–303, is a complex stream-of-consciousness novel, which portrays a Qajar prince as a symbol of the diminishing Iranian aristocracy and monarchy.

33. Golshiri, *Keristin va Kid*, p. 91.

34. Ibid., p. 95. Baron Julius de Reuter was a British subject who was granted a concession in 1872 by the Iranian government to set up railways, roads, and irrigation systems and to establish a national bank. Under pressure from the Russians, this concession was canceled. Later, in 1889, he established the Imperial Bank of Persia. William Knox d'Arcy was an Australian who was granted a sixty-year concession in 1901 to explore natural gas and petroleum throughout most of Iran. Colonel Henry Smyth was a member of the British Military Mission to Iran after World War I. Upon the departure of the Russians from Iran, the British took over the Cossack Division. According to Houshang Sabahi, in his *British Policy in Persia: 1918-1925*, pp. 52, 228, Smyth apparently had prior knowledge of the coup d'etat that overthrew the Qajar Dynasty and placed Reza Khan (Reza Shah) in power in Iran, and was in fact cooperating with the conspirators. All of these names would conjure up negative images for many educated Iranians.

6. Post-Revolutionary Reflections

1. Although not central to my argument regarding the perception of modern Iranian writers, it should be noted that the tradition of the Twelver Shi'ites has considered non-believers—among them Christians and, hence, Westerners—as ritually unclean and therefore untouchable, at least since the sixteenth century. For a historical account of the perceptions of Iranian Moslems, see Roger Savory, "Muslim Perceptions of the West: Iran" in *As Others See Us: Mutual Perceptions, East and West*, ed. Bernard Lewis, Edmund Leites, and Margaret Case, in *Comparative Civilizations Review* 13 (Fall 1985) and 14 (Spring 1986):73–89.

2. On censorship, see Baqer Mo'meni, "Sansur va Avarez-e Nashi az An" [Censorship and Its Symptoms], in *Dah Shab*, comp. Naser Mo'azzen, pp. 253-265; M. R. Ghanoonparvar, "Literary Ambiguity," in *Prophets of Doom: Literature as a Socio-Political Phenomenon in Modern Iran*, pp. 149–177; Ahmad Karimi-Hakkak, "Protest and Perish: A History of the Writers' Association of Iran," *Iranian Studies* 18 (Spring–Autumn 1985):189–229.

3. Ehsan Naraqi, *Ghorbat-e Gharb*, 4th ed.

4. The more outspoken Iranians who advocated emulation of the West were Mirza Malkom Khan Nazemoddowleh, a prominent official during the Qajar period, and Hasan Taqizadeh, an influential figure in the Iranian Constitutional Revolution (1906–911). The latter is quoted by E. G. Browne in his *A History of Persia*, vol. 4, p. 486, as having declared that Iran must become Europeanized in body and soul. However, he later modified his beliefs, no longer supporting blind acceptance of all things Western.

5. Naraqi summarizes these observations in his preface, pp. 1–8.

6. Ahmad Kasravi, *A'in* (Tehran: 1311 [1932/33], pp. 3–7.

7. For an overview of Kasravi's observations about the West, see M. A. Jazayery, "Kasravi va Barkhord-e Sharq ba Gharb," *Iran Nameh* 8, no. 3 (Summer 1990):391–410. The only available works of Kasravi in English translation are *"On Islam"* and *"Shi'ism"*, trans. M. R. Ghanoonparvar, which includes an introductory article by M. A. Jazayery, "Kasravi, Iconoclastic Thinker of Twentieth-Century Iran," pp. 1–53.

8. These books were: Reza Baraheni, *God's Shadow: Prison Poems*, with David St. John and Michael Henderson, and *The Crowned Cannibals: Writings on Repression in Iran*.

9. Reza Baraheni, *Avaz-e Koshtegan*.

10. Reza Baraheni, *Razha-ye Sarzamin-e Man*, vols. 1 and 2.

11. Ibid., vol. 1, p. 16.

12. Ibid.

13. Ibid., p. 17.

14. Ibid., pp. 17–18.

15. Ibid., pp. 25–26.

16. Ibid., p. 26.

17. Ibid.

18. Ibid., pp. 28–29.

19. Ibid., p. 44.

20. Ibid., p. 62.

21. Ibid.

22. Ibid., p. 65.

23. Ibid., pp. 68–69.

24. Ibid., p. 81.
25. Ibid., pp. 94–95.
26. Ibid., p. 95.
27. Ibid., p. 213.
28. Manoucher Parvin, *Cry for My Revolution, Iran.*
29. Ibid., p. 385.
30. Khosrow Nasimi, *Raqs-e Ranj.*
31. Ibid., p. 4.
32. Ibid., p. 5.
33. Ibid., p. 315.
34. Faramarz Talebi, *Bargha'i az Fasl-e Khun,* p. 15.
35. Ibid., p. 31.
36. Ibid., p. 17.
37. Ali Kamali, *Enqelab.*
38. Mahshid Amirshahy, *Dar Hazar.*
39. Amirshahy was educated in England and has lived in Europe since the early 1980s.
40. Amirshahy, p. 40.
41. Ibid., p. 45.
42. Ibid., p. 182.
43. Moniru Ravanipur, *Ahl-e Gharq.*
44. Some critics have argued that in *Ahl-e Gharq,* Ravanipur is under the influence of Latin American writers, particularly Gabriel García Márquez. But it can also be argued that *Ahl-e Gharq* is a natural development of fiction writing in Iran, bearing perhaps influences of several Iranian writers of the previous two or three decades. Nevertheless, in her work, Ravanipur displays a great degree of originality, which makes her novel unique not only as a story with a new subject matter but in terms of style of presentation. See M. R. Ghanoonparvar, "Dami ba Ahl-e Gharq," *Iranshenasi* (Summer 1992).
45. Ravanipur, pp. 127–128.

46. Ibid., p. 334.
47. Ibid., p. 335.
48. Ibid. For a discussion of *Ahl-e Gharq* as a novel of "magical realism" and its political ramifications, see Nasrin Rahimieh, "Submersed in Dialect: Magical Realism in 'Ahl-e Qarq'," paper presented at the 1991 Annual Meeting of the Middle East Studies Association of North America in Washington, D.C. (forthcoming in *Iranian Studies*).
49. Ravanipur, p. 397.
50. "Goft-o Gu ba Hushang Golshiri," *Ayandegan* (August 6, 1979 [15 Mordad 1358]), pp. 6 and 10. In addition, see M. R. Ghanoonparvar, "Hushang Golshiri and Post-Pahlavi Concerns of the Iranian Writer of Fiction," *Iranian Studies* 18 (Spring, Autumn 1985): 349–373.
51. Esmail Fassih, *Sorayya dar Eghma,* 3d ed.
52. All citations from this novel are from the English translation: Esmail Fassih, *Sorraya in a Coma.* It is worthy of note that the anonymous translator has chosen an aberrant spelling of the name Sorayya in this work.
53. See Chapter 3, "The West in Contrast."
54. Fassih, *Sorraya in a Coma,* p. 260. Fassih himself apparently had a hand in the English translation; hence, the misspelling of Zangaro as Zangaroo, to rhyme with kangaroo, may be intentional, evoking the familiar phrase "kangaroo court" in English. The Iran that he describes in the passage quoted here could very well be an extension of this image.
55. Ibid., p. 188. For a more detailed analysis of this novel, see

Faridoun Farrokh and M. R. Ghanoonparvar, "Portraits in Exile in the Fiction of Esma'il Fassih and Goli Taraghi" in Asghar Fathi, ed., *Iranian Refugees and Exiles since Khomeini*, pp. 281–293.

56. These travel diaries are discussed in Chapter 2, "Understanding the Unknown."

57. Mahmud Golabdarreh'i, *Dal*, 2d ed.

58. Ibid., p. 14.

59. Ibid., p. 103.

60. Ibid., p. 317.

61. Ibid., p. 319.

7. Conclusion: On the Mirror and the Image Makers

1. On fiction, see for example, Jamal Mirsadeqi, *Qesseh, Dastan-e Kutah, Roman*, pp. 265–266, and "Negahi Kutah beh Dastannevisi-ye Mo'aser-e Iran," *Sokhan* 26, no. 9 (August–September 1978):913–931.

On poetry, see Ali Asghar Hekmat, "She'r-e Farsi dar Asr-e Mo'aser," in *Nakhostin Kongereh-ye Nevisandegan-e Iran*, pp. 11–29; Hamid Zarrinkub, *Cheshmandaz-e She'r-e No-ye Farsi*, pp. 7–45.

On drama, see Jamshid Malekpur, *Adabiyyat-e Namayeshi dar Iran*, vol. 2; M. R. Ghanoonparvar, "Introduction," in *Iranian Drama: An Anthology*, comp. and ed. M. R. Ghanoonparvar with John Green, pp. ix–xxix.

2. On these changes, see Leonardo P. Alishan's introductory essay to "Ten Poems by Nima Yushij," *Literature East and West* 20 (1976):21–25; and Ahmad Karimi-Hakkak's introduction to *An Anthology of Modern Persian Poetry*.

3. Mohammad Ali Jamalzadeh, "Dibacheh," *Yeki Bud, Yeki Nabud*,

10th ed., p. 1. For an English translation, see Haideh Dargahi, "The Shaping of the Modern Persian Short Story: Jamalzadih's 'Preface' to *Yiki Bud, Yiki Nabud*," *The Literary Review* 18 (1974):18-24.

4. Jamalzadeh, p. 5.

5. On the effects of translation, see Hasan Abedini, *Sad Sal Dastan-nevisi dar Iran, 1253-1342 [1874-1963]*, vol. 1, 2d ed., pp. 117–121, 201–206. The volume also includes percentages of translations of books published in Iran. Also see, M. A. Jazayery, "Recent Persian Literature: Observations on Themes and Tendencies," *Review of National Literatures* 2, no. 1 (1971):-11–28.

6. In recent years university students in Iran have become more receptive to research on modern Persian literature. Several students in Iran have corresponded with me about writing their theses on contemporary works, even on the most recently published novels.

7. Reza Baraheni, *Kimiya va Khak*, 2d ed., p. 62.

8. Ibid., p. 52. *Ardavirafnameh* is a book written in Pahlavi which describes the ascension of Ardaviraf, a high-ranking Zoroastrian priest.

9. Jalal Matini, former head of the Persian Literature Department and chancellor of the University of Mashhad, addressing a Persian-speaking audience at the "Nezami Congress: On the Occasion of the 850th Anniversary of the Celebrated Twelfth-Century Persian Poet" at the University of California at Los Angeles in May 1991, made a similar observation about the prominence given Western

scholarship even in a field such as
Persian literature, in which
Iranians boast of being experts.

10. A similar argument, albeit
in a different context, is set forth
by Michael Beard in his *Hedayat's
"Blind Owl" as a Western Novel*,
who states: "The novel, like the

short story, is a borrowed Western
innovation" (p. 9).

11. Ibid., p. 4. Sadeq
Hedayat's *Buf-e Kur* is still the
best-known Iranian novel. For an
English translation, see *The Blind
Owl*, trans. D. P. Costello.

SELECTED BIBLIOGRAPHY

Persian Works in English Translation

Alavi, Bozorg. *Her Eyes.* Translated by John O'Kane. Lanham, Md.: University Press of America, 1989.

———. *Scrap Papers from Prison: The Prison Papers of Bozorg Alavi, A Literary Odyssey.* Translated by Donné Raffat. Syracuse: Syracuse University Press, 1985.

Al-e Ahmad, Jalal. *Gharbzadegi (Weststruckness).* Translated by John Green and Ahmad Alizadeh. Lexington, Ky.: Mazda Publishers, 1982.

———. *Lost in the Crowd.* Translated by John Green, Ahmad Alizadeh, et al. Washington, D.C.: Three Continents Press, 1985.

———. *Plagued by the West (Gharbzadegi).* Translated by Paul Sprachman. Delmar, N.Y.: Caravan Books, 1982.

———. *The School Principal.* Translated by John K. Newton. Minneapolis and Chicago: Bibliotheca Islamica, 1974.

Amirshahy, Mahshid. "String of Beads." Translated by Michael Beard. *Edibiyat* 3 (1978):1–9.

Attar, Farid ud-Din. *The Conference of the Birds.* Translated by Afkham Darbandi and Dick Davis. New York: Penguin Books, 1984.

Baraheni, Reza. *The Crowned Cannibals: Writings on Repression in Iran.* New York: Vintage Books, 1977.

———, with David St. John and Michael Henderson. *God's Shadow: Prison Poems.* Bloomington: Indiana University Press, 1976.

———. *The Infernal Days of Aqa-ye Ayaz.* Translated by Carter Bryant. In "Reza Baraheni's 'The Infernal Days of Aqa-ye Ayaz': A Translation and Critical Introduction." PhD diss. University of Texas at Austin, 1982:112–726.

Behrangi, Samad. *The Little Black Fish and Other Modern Persian Short Stories*. Translated by Mary and Eric Hooglund. Washington, D.C.: Three Continents Press, 1976.

Chubak, Sadeq. *An Anthology*. Translated and edited by F. R. C. Bagley. Delmar, N.Y.: Caravan Books, 1982.

———. "The Baboon Whose Buffoon Was Dead." Translated by Peter W. Avery. *New World Writing* 11 (1957):14–24.

———. "The Cage" and "The Wooden Horse." Translated by L. Kroutiova, Vera Kubickova, and I. Lewit. *New Orient* 4 (1965):148–152.

———. "Justice" and "Flowers of Flesh." Translated by John Limbert. *Iranian Studies* 1 (1968):113–119. Also translated as "Inquest" by H. D. Law. In *Life and Letters and the London Mercury* 63 (1949):230–232.

———. "Monsieur Elias." Translated by William L. Hanaway, Jr. *The Literary Review* 18 (1974):61–68.

———. *The Patient Stone*. Translated by M. R. Ghanoonparvar. Costa Mesa, Calif.: Mazda Publishers, 1989.

———. "Yahya." Translated by H. D. Law. *Life and Letters and the London Mercury* 63 (1949):228–229.

Daneshvar, Simin. *Daneshvar's Playhouse*. Translated by Maryam Mafi. Washington, D.C.: Mage Publishers, 1989.

———. *Savushun: A Novel About Iran*. Translated by M. R. Ghanoonparvar. Washington, D.C.: Mage Publishers, 1990.

E'tesami, Parvin. *A Nightingale's Lament*. Translated by Heshmat Moayyad and A. Margaret Arent Madelung. Lexington, Ky.: Mazda Publishers, 1985.

Farrokhzad, Forugh. *Another Birth: Selected Poems of Forugh Farrokhzad*. Translated by Hasan Javadi and Susan Sallee. Emeryville, Calif.: Albany Press, 1981.

———. *Bride of Acacia*. Translated by Jascha Kessler and Amin Banani. Delmar, N.Y.: Caravan Books, 1982.

Fassih, Esmail. *Sorraya in a Coma*. Translator anonymous. London: Zed Books, 1985.

Ghanoonparvar, M. R., comp. and ed. with John Green. *Iranian Drama: An Anthology*. Costa Mesa, Calif: Mazda Publishers, 1989.

Golestan, Ebrahim. "Bend of the Road." Translated by Karim Emami. *Kayhan International Supplement* (October 7, 1976):10–11.

Golshiri, Hushang. "Behind the Thin Branches of the Screen." Translated by M. R. Ghanoonparvar. *Artful Dodge* 12, 13 (Fall 1985):115–117.

————. *Prince Ehtejab.* Translated by Minoo R. Buffington. Literature East and West 20 (1976):250–303.

Hamalian, Leo, and John D. Yohannan, eds. "Persian Literature." *New Writing from the Middle East.* New York: Mentor, 1978. [Includes selections of Persian prose fiction, poetry, and drama.]

Hasan, Hadi, trans. *A Golden Treasury of Persian Poetry.* Delhi: Ministry of Information and Broadcasting, 1966.

Hedayat, Sadeq. *The Blind Owl.* Translated by D. P. Costello. New York: Grove Press, Inc., 1957; New York: Evergreen, 1969.

————. *"The Blind Owl" and Other Hedayat Stories.* Compiled by Carol L. Sayers. Edited by Russell P. Christensen. Minneapolis: Sorayya Publishers, 1984.

————. *Haji Agha: Portrait of an Iranian Confidence Man.* Translated by G. M. Wickens. Austin: Center for Middle Eastern Studies, University of Texas, 1979.

————. *Sadeq Hedayat: An Anthology.* Edited by Ehsan Yarshater. Boulder: Westview Press, 1979.

————. "The Mongol's Shadow." Translated by Donald S. Shojai. *Chicago Review* 20 (1969):95–104.

————. *Sadeq's Omnibus: A Collection of Short Stories.* Translated by Siavosh Danesh. Tehran: Mehre Danesh, 1972.

————. "Three Drops of Blood." Translated by Thomas M. Ricks. *Iranian Studies* 3 (1970):104–114.

Hillmann, Michael, comp. and ed. *Iranian Society: An Anthology of Writings by Jalal Al-e Ahmad.* Lexington, Ky.: Mazda Publishers, 1982.

————, ed. *Major Voices in Contemporary Persian Literature. Literature East and West* 20 (1976).

Irani, Manuchehr. *King of the Benighted.* Translated by Abbas Milani. Washington, D.C.: Mage Publishers, 1990.

Jafari, Javad. *The Last Love of the Princess.* Translated by M. R. Ghanoonparvar. Bethlehem, Pa.: Design and Art Books, 1989.

Jamalzadeh, Mohammad Ali. *Isfahan Is Half the World: Memories of a Persian Boyhood.* Translated by W. L. Heston. Princeton: Princeton University Press, 1983.

————. *Once Upon a Time.* Translated by Heshmat Moayyad and Paul Sprachman. New York: Bibliotheca Persica, 1985.

Karimi-Hakkak, Ahmad, comp. and trans. *An Anthology of Modern Persian Poetry.* Boulder: Westview Press, 1978.

Kasravi, Ahmad. *"On Islam" and "Shi'ism"*. Translated by M. R. Ghanoonparvar. Introduction by M. A. Jazayery. Costa Mesa, Calif.: Mazda Publishers, 1990.

Lahuti, Mohammad Reza, ed. *Short Stories*. Translated by Saeed Nabavi. Tehran: Cultural Institute for Art Development, 1989.

Life and Letters 63 (December 1979):196–270. [Includes selections of Persian poetry and prose fiction.]

The Literary Review 18 (Fall 1976). [Includes selections of Persian poetry and prose fiction.]

Moayyad, Heshmat, ed. *Stories from Iran: A Chicago Anthology, 1921–1991.* Washington, D.C.: Mage Publishers, 1991.

Modarressi, Taghi. *The Pilgrim's Rules of Etiquette*. Translated by the author. New York: Doubleday, 1989.

Mofid, Bizhan. *The Butterfly*. Translated by Don Laffoon. Anchorage, Ky.: Anchorage Press, 1974.

Naderpur, Nader. *False Dawn*. Translated by Michael C. Hillmann. *Literature East and West* 22 (1986).

Sadeqi, Bahram. "Imminent." Translated by Karim Emami. *Kayhan International Supplement*, September 2, 1965.

Sa'di. *Gulistan or Flower Garden*. Translated by James Ross. London: Walter Scott, Ltd., 1823), pp. 150–151.

———. *Morals Pointed and Tales Adorned*. Translated by G. M. Wickens. Leiden: E. J. Brill, 1974.

Sa'edi, Gholamhoseyn. *The Cow: A Screenplay*. Translated by Mohsen Ghadessy. *Iranian Studies* 18 (1985):257–323.

———. *Dandil: Stories from Iranian Life*. Translated by Robert Campbell, Hasan Javadi, and Julie S. Meisami. New York: Random House, 1981.

———. *Fear and Trembling*. Translated by Minoo Southgate. Washington, D.C.: Three Continents Press, 1984.

———. "The Wedding." Translated by Jerome W. Clinton. *Iranian Studies* 8 (1975):2–47.

Ahmad Shamlu. "Six Poems." Translated by David Anderson and Jerome W. Clinton. *Edebiyat* 3 (1978):23–26.

Sholevar, Bahman. *The Night's Journey and the Coming of the Messiah*. Translated by the author. Philadelphia: Concourse Press, 1984.

Southgate, Minoo S., ed. and trans. *Modern Persian Short Stories*. Washington, D.C.: Three Continents Press, 1980.

Sullivan, Soraya Paknazar, trans. *Stories by Iranian Women Since the Revolution*. Austin: Center for Middle Eastern Studies, University of Texas, 1991.

Yushij, Nima. "The Cock Crows." Translated by Munibar Rahman. *Edebiyat* 2 (1977):41–42.

Sources in English

Abrahamian, Ervand. *Iran between Two Revolutions.* Princeton: Princeton University Press, 1982.

Algar, Hamid. *Mirza Malkum Khan: A Study in the History of Iranian Modernism.* Berkeley: University of California Press, 1973.

Alishan, Leonardo P. Introduction to "Teh Poems by Nima Yushij." *Literature East and West* 20 (1976):21–25.

Bamdad, Badr ol-Moluk. *From Darkness into Light: Women's Emancipation in Iran.* Edited and translated by F. R. C. Bagley. Hicksville, N.Y.: Exposition Press, 1977.

Banani, Amin. *The Modernization of Iran (1921–1941).* Stanford: Stanford University Press, 1961.

Beard, Michael. *Hedayat's "Blind Owl" as a Western Novel.* Princeton: Princeton University Press, 1990.

Boroujerdi, Mehrzad. *Iranian Intellectuals and the West: A Study in Orientalism in Reverse.* Albany: SUNY, 1993.

Bosworth, Edmond, and Carole Hillenbrand, eds. *Qajar Iran: Political, Social, and Cultural Change, 1800–1925.* Costa Mesa, Calif.: Mazda Publishers, 1992; Edinburgh: Edinburgh University Press, 1983.

Browne, E. G. *A History of Persia,* vol. 4. Cambridge: Cambridge University Press, 1924.

———. *The Persian Revolution of 1905–1909.* Cambridge: Cambridge University Press, 1910.

Dargahi, Haideh. "The Shaping of the Modern Persian Short Story: Jamalzadih's 'Preface' to *Yiki Bud, Yiki Nabud*." *The Literary Review* 18 (1974):18–24.

Denny, Frederick Mathewson. *An Introduction to Islam.* New York: MacMillan Publishing Company, 1985.

Diba, Farhad. *Mossadegh: A Political Biography.* London, Sydney, Dover, and New Hampshire: Croom Helm, 1986.

Farmayan, Hafez F. "Observations on Sources for the Study of Nineteenth- and Twentieth-Century Iranian History." *International Journal of Middle East Studies* 5 (January 1974):32–49.

————, and Elton Daniel, ed. and trans. *A Shi'ite Pilgrimage to Mecca, 1885–1886: The Safarnameh of Mirza Mohammad Hosayn Farahani.* Austin: University of Texas Press, 1990.

Farrokh, Faridoun, with M. R. Ghanoonparvar. "Portraits in Exile in the Fiction of Esma'il Fassih and Goli Taraghi." *Iranian Refugees and Exiles since Khomeini.* Ed. Asghar Fathi. Costa Mesa, Calif.: Mazda Publishers, 1991. Pp. 280–293.

Fathi, Asghar, ed. *Iranian Refugees and Exiles since Khomeini.* Costa Mesa, California: Mazda Publishers, 1991.

Floor, William F. "The Political Role of the Lutis." In *Modern Iran: The Dialectics of Change and Continuity,* edited by Michael Bonine and Nikki Keddie. New York: SUNY, 1981.

Ghanoonparvar, M. R. "Generic Experimentation and Social Content in Nader Ebrahimi's *Ten Short Stories. Iranian Studies* 15, nos. 1–4 (1982):129–154.

————. "Hushang Golshiri and Post-Pahlavi Concerns of the Iranian Writer of Fiction." *Iranian Studies* 18 (Spring, Autumn 1985):349–373.

————. "On *Savushun* and Simin Daneshvar's Contribution to Persian Fiction." *Iranshenasi* 3 (Winter 1992):77–88.

————. *Prophets of Doom: Literature as a Socio-Political Phenomenon in Modern Iran.* Lanham, Md.: University Press of America, 1984.

Göçek, Fatma Müge. *East Encounters West: France and the Ottoman Empire in the Eighteenth Century.* New York: Oxford University Press, 1987.

Hoveyda, Fereydoun. *The Fall of the Shah.* New York: Simon and Schuster, 1980.

Javadi, Hasan. *Satire in Persian Literature.* London and Toronto: Associated University Presses, 1988.

Jazayery, M. A. "Recent Persian Literature: Observations on Themes and Tendencies." *Review of National Literatures* 2, no. 1 (1971):11–28.

Kamshad, Hassan. *Modern Persian Prose Literature.* Cambridge: Cambridge University Press, 1966.

Karimi-Hakkak, Ahmad. Review of a translation of Jamalzadeh's *Isfahan Is Half the World.* In *Iranian Studies* 18 (Spring–Autumn 1985):423–427.

Kazemzadeh, Firuz. *Russia and Britain in Persia, 1864–1914.* Chicago: University of Chicago Press, 1971.

Karimi-Hakkak, Ahmad, "Protest and Perish: A History of the Writers' Association of Iran." *Iranian Studies* 18 (Spring–Autumn 1985):189–229.

Keddie, Nikki R. *Roots of Revolution: An Interpretive History of Modern Iran.* New Haven: Yale University Press, 1981.

Lewis, Bernard, Edmund Leites, and Margaret Case, eds. *As Others See Us: Mutual Perceptions, East and West.* In *Comparative Civilizations Review* 13 (Fall 1985) and 14 (Spring 1986).

Millspaugh, Arthur Chester. *Americans in Persia.* Reprint. New York: Da Capo Press, 1976.

Morier, James. *The Adventures of Hajji Baba of Ispahan.* Edited by C. J. Wills. London: Laurence and Bullen, 1897.

Naficy, Hamid. "Iranian Writers, the Iranian Cinema, and the Case of *Dash Akol.*" *Iranian Studies* 18, nos. 2–4 (Spring–Autumn 1985):231–251.

Parvin, Manoucher. *Cry for My Revolution, Iran.* Costa Mesa, Calif.: Mazda Publishers, 1987.

Rahimieh, Nasrin. *Oriental Responses to the West: Comparative Essays in Select Writers from the Muslim World.* Leiden and New York: E. J. Brill, 1990.

Rajaee, Farhang. *Islamic Values and World View: Khomeyni on Man, the State and International Politics.* Lanham, Md.: University Press of America, 1983.

Ramazani, R. K. *The United States and Iran: The Patterns of Influence.* New York: Praeger, 1982.

Roosevelt, Kermit. *Countercoup: The Struggle for the Control of Iran.* New York: McGraw-Hill, 1979.

Rukni Musawi Lari, Sayid Mujtaba. *Western Civilization Through Muslim Eyes.* Translated by F. J. Goulding. Qum, Iran: n.p., 1977.

Sabahi, Houshang. *British Policy in Persia: 1918–1925.* London: Frank Cass, 1990.

Said, Edward W. *Orientalism.* New York: Vintage, 1978.

Sharifi, Naser. *Cataloging Persian Works.* Chicago: American Library Association, 1959.

Shuster, William Morgan. *The Strangling of Persia.* New York: The Century Company, 1912.

Tavakoli-Targhi, Mohamad. *Women of the West Imagined: Occidentalism and Exotic Europeans.* Berkeley: University of California Press, 1993.

Winks, Robin W., and James R. Rush. *Asia in Western Fiction.* Honolulu: University of Hawaii Press, 1990.

Yarshater, Ehsan, ed. *Persian Literature.* [New York]: Bibliotheca Persica, 1988.

Sources in Persian

Abedini, Hasan. *Sad Sal Dastannevisi dar Iran.* Vol. 1, 2d ed.:
1253–1342 [1874–1963]. Tehran: Nashr-e Tandar, 1368 [1989].
———. *Sad Sal Dastannevisi dar Iran.* Vol. 2, 2d ed.: 1342–1357
[1963–1979]. Tehran: Nashr-e Tandar, 1369 [1990].
Abu Taleb Khan, Mirza. *Masir-e Talebi ya Safarnameh-ye Mirza
Abu Taleb Khan.* 2d ed. Edited by Hoseyn Khadiv-Jam.
Tehran: Sazman-e Entesharat va Amuzesh-e Enqelab-e
Eslami, 1363 [1984].
Afghani, Ali Mohammad. *Doktor Baktash.* Tehran: Entesharat-e
Negah, 1364 [1985].
Alavi, Bozorg. *Chashmhayash.* Tehran: Entesharat-e Javidan,
1357 [1978].
Alavi-Shirazi, Mirza Mohammad Hadi. *Safarnameh-ye Mirza Abol
Hasan Khan Shirazi (Ilchi) be Rusiyyeh.* Tehran: Donya-ye
Ketab, 1363 [1984].
Al-e Ahmad, Jalal. *Gharbzadegi.* Reprint. Tehran: Entesharat-e
Ravaq, 1356 [1977].
———. *Modir-e Madreseh.* 7th ed. Tehran: Amir Kabir, 1358
[1979].
———. *Panj Dastan.* 4th ed. Tehran: Entesharat-e Ravaq, 1355
[1976].
———. *Sargozasht-e Kanduha.* 5th ed. Tehran: Entesharat-e
Javidan, 1355 [1976].
Amirshahy, Mahshid. *Dar Hazar.* London: Cushing-Malloy,
1366 [1987].
Attar-Neyshaburi, Sheykh Faridoddin Mohammad. *Manteq ot-
Teyr.* 4th ed. Edited by Seyyed Sadeq Gowharin. Tehran:
Sherkat-e Entesharat-e Elmi va Farhangi, 1365 [1986].
Baraheni, Reza. *Avaz-e Koshtegan.* Tehran: Nashr-e No, 1362
[1983].
———. *Kimiya va Khak.* 2d ed. Tehran: Nashr-e Morgh-e
Amin, 1366 [1987].
———. *Qessehnevisi.* 2d ed. Tehran: Sazman-e Entesharat-e
Ashrafi, 1348 [1969].
———. *Razha-ye Sarzamin-e Man.* Vols. 1 and 2. Tehran:
Nashr-e Moghan, 1366 [1987].
Bastani-Parizi, Mohammad Ebrahim. *Az Pariz ta Paris: Haft
Shahr, Haft Jush, Haft Rang.* Tehran: Entesharat-e Amir
Kabir, 1352 [1973].
Behnam, Jamshid. "Dar Bareh-ye Tajaddod-e Iran (I)." *Iran
Nameh* 8 (Summer 1990):347–374.

Boroujerdi, Mehrzad. "Gharbzadegi va Sharqshenasi-ye Varuneh." *Iran Nameh* 8 (Summer 1990):375–410.

Chubak, Sadeq. *Cheragh-e Akhar*. Tehran: Entesharat-e Elmi, 1345 [1966].

———. *Tangsir*. 2d ed. Tehran: Javidan, 1347 [1968].

Daneshvar, Simin. *Savushun*. 9th ed. Tehran: Kharazmi, 1357 [1978].

———. *Shahri Chun Behesht*. 2d ed. Tehran: Ketab-e Mowj, 1354 [1975].

Dehbashi, Ali, ed. *Safarnameh-ye Haj Sayyah beh Farang*. Tehran: Nashr-e Nasher, 1363 [1984].

Eslami-Nodushan, Mohammad Ali. *Azadi-ye Mojassameh: Darbareh-ye Eyalat-e Mottahedeh-ye Amrika*. Tehran: Entesharat-e Tus, 1356 [1977].

———. *Goftim-o Nagoftim*. Tehran:Entesharat-e Yazdan, 1362 [1983].

Fassih, Esmail. *Sorayya dar Eghma*. 3d ed. Tehran: Nashr-e No, 1364 [1985].

Ghanoonparvar, M. R. "Ba Neqab-e Siyah: Tahlili az Seh Dastan-e Kutah-e Simin Daneshvar." *Nimeye-Digar* 8 (Fall 1988):165–179.

———. "Dami ba Ahl-e Gharq." *Iranshenasi* (Summer 1992).

———. "Kand va Kavi dar *Zanan bedun-e Mardan*." *Iran Nameh* 9, no. 4 (Autumn 1991):690–699.

———. "Nava-ye Naqqal dar *Klidar*." *Fasl-e Ketab* 2 (Summer 1991):96–101.

———. "Neveshtan-e Darmani dar *Buf-e Kur*." *Kelk* 7 (Fall 1990):57–64.

———. "Oruj-e Yek Yaghi: Rahbord-e Ravayat dar *Klidar*." *Iran Nameh* 7 (Winter 1989):355–366.

Golabdarreh'i, Mahmud. *Dal*. 2d ed. [Tehran]: Katibeh, 1366 [1987].

Golshiri, Hushang. *Jobbehkhaneh*. Tehran: Ketab-e Tehran, 1362 [1983].

———. *Keristin va Kid*. 2d ed. Tehran: Ketab-e Zaman, 2536 [1977].

———. *Shazdeh Ehtejab*. 7th ed. Tehran: Entesharat-e Qoqnus, 1358 [1979].

Hariri, Naser. *Honar va Adabiyyat-e Emruz*. Babol: Ketabsara-ye Babol, 1366 [1987].

Hedayat, Sadeq. *Buf-e Kur*. 14th ed. Tehran: Amir Kabir, 1352 [1973].

————. *Karvan-e Eslam: Al-Be'sat ol-Eslamiyyah Ela al- Belad al-Faranjiyyah.* 2d ed. Paris: Organisation des Mouvements Nationalistes des Universitaires, Chercheurs, et Intellectuels Iraniens, 1982.

————. "Le Magic en Perse" (in French). Reprinted in *Neveshtehha-ye Parakandeh.* Tehran: Amir Kabir, 1365 [1986/1987].

————. *Parvin Dokhtar-e Sasan.* 3d ed. Tehran: Amir Kabir, 1342 [1963].

————. *Sag-e Velgard.* Tehran: Entesharat-e Javidan, 1354 [1975/6].

————. *Sayeh Rowshan.* 5th ed. Tehran: Amir Kabir, 1342 [1963].

————. *Seh Qatreh Khun.* 8th ed. Tehran: Ketabha-ye Parastu, 1344 [1965].

————. *Tup-e Morvari.* Edited by Iraj Bashiri. Costa Mesa, CA: Mazda Publishers, 1986.

Hejazi, Mohammad. *Sereshk.* Tehran: Entesharat-e Ebn-e Sina, 1332 [1953].

Hekmat, Ali Asghar. "She'r-e Farsi dar Asr-e Mo'aser." In *Nakhostin Kongereh-ye Nevisandegan-e Iran.* Tehran: Anjoman-e Ravabet-e Farhangi-ye Iran va Ettehad-e Jamahir-e Showravi-ye Sosiyalisti, 1947. Pp. 11–29.

Jamalzadeh, Mohammad Ali. *Yeki Bud, Yeki Nabud.* 10th ed. Tehran: Kanun-e Ma'refat, 2537 [1978].

Jazayery, M. A. "Kasravi va Barkhord-e Sharq ba Gharb." *Iran Nameh* 8, no.3 (Summer 1990):391–410.

Kamali, Ali. *Enqelab.* Tehran: Mo'asseseh-ye Mas'ud, 1358 [1979].

Kasravi, Ahmad. *A'in.* Tehran: n.p., 1311 [1932/1933].

Khanshaqaqi, Hoseynqoli, ed. *Khaterat-e Montahen ol-Dowleh.* 2d ed. Tehran: Entesharat-e Amir Kabir, 1362 [1983].

Madani, Hoseyn. *Esmal dar Niyuyork.* Vol. 1, 4th ed. Tehran: Entesharat-e Sharq, 1333 [1954].

————. *Esmal dar Niyuyork.* Vol. 2, 2d ed. Tehran: Entesharat-e Amir Kabir, 1334 [1955].

————. *Esmal dar Niyuyork.* Vol. 3, 2d ed. Tehran: Entesharat-e Amir Kabir, n.d.

Mahdavi, Abdolreza Hushang. *Tarikh-e Ravabet-e Khareji-ye Iran az Ebteda-ye Dowran-e Safavi-ye ta Payan-e Jang-e Jahani-ye Dovvom.* 3d ed. Tehran: Entesharat-e Amir Kabir, 1364 [1985].

Mahmud, Ahmad. *Hamsayehha.* 4th ed. Tehran: Entesharat-e Amir Kabir, 2537 [1978].

Malekpur, Jamshid. *Adabiyyat-e Namayeshi dar Iran.* Vol. 2. Tehran: Entesharat-e Tus, 1363 [1984/1985].

Maragheh'i, Zeynol'abeddin. *Siyahatnameh-ye Ebrahim Beyg.* Tehran: Ketabha-ye Sadaf, 1344 [1965].

Mas'ud, Mohammad. *Golha-i keh dar Jahannam Miruyad.* Tehran: Entesharat-e Javidan, 2537 [1978].

Mirsadeqi, Jamal, ed. *Dastanha-ye No.* Tehran: Entesharat-e Shabahang, 1366 [1987].

———. "Negahi Kutah beh Dastannevisi-ye Mo'aser-e Iran." *Sokhan* 26, no. 9 (August–September 1978):913–931.

———. *Qesseh, Dastan-e Kutah, Roman.* Tehran: Entesharat-e Agah, 1360 [1981].

Mo'azzen, Naser, comp. *Dah Shab.* Tehran: Amir Kabir, 2537 [1978].

Morsalvand, Hasan. *Heyratnameh: Safarnameh-ye Abolhasan Khan Ilchi beh Landan.* Tehran: Mo'asseh-ye Khadamat-e Farhangi-ye Rasa, 1364 [1986].

Moshiri, Mohammad, ed. *Safarnameh-ye Ebrahim Sahhafbashi-Tehrani.* Tehran: Sherkat-e Mo'allefan va Motarjeman-e Iran, 2537 [1978].

Naraqi, Ehsan. *Ghorbat-e Gharb.* 4th ed. Tehran: Amir Kabir, 2536 [1977].

Nasimi, Khosrow. *Raqs-e Ranj.* Tehran: Entesharat-e Kamangir, 1359 [1981].

Nateq, Homa. "Farang va Farangma'abi va Resaleh-ye Enteqadi-ye Sheykh va Shoyukh." *Zaman-e No* 12 (1986):49–67.

Navvab-Safa, Esma'il. *Sharh-e Hal-e Farhad Mirza Mo'tamed od-Dowleh.* Tehran: Entesharat-e Zavvar, 1366 [1987].

Pezeshkzad, Iraj. *Da'ijan Napel'on.* 12th ed. London: Paka Print, 1357 [1978].

Pirzadeh-Na'ini, Mohammad. *Safarnameh-ye Haji Pirzadeh: Az Tehran ta Landan.* Vol. 1, 2d ed. Edited by Hafez F. Farmayan. Tehran: Entesharat-e Babak, 1360 [1981].

———. *Safarnameh-ye Haji Pirzadeh: Az Landan ta Esfahan.* Vol. 2, 2d ed. Edited by Hafez F. Farmayan. Tehran: Entesharat-e Babak, 1360 [1981].

Qajar, Mozaffaroddin Shah. *Safarnameh-ye Farangestan: Safar-e Avval.* 2d ed. Edited by Amir Shirazi. Tehran: Entesharat-e Sharq, 1363 [1984].

Qajar, Naseroddin Shah. *Safarnameh-ye Farangestan: Safar-e Dovvom.* 2d ed. Tehran: Entesharat-e Sharq, 1363 [1984].

Qobadiyani-Marvazi, Naser ebn Khosrow. *Safarnameh-ye Naser Khosrow*. 2d ed. Edited by Nader Vazinpur. Tehran: Ketabha-ye Jibi, 1354 [1975].

Rahimi, Reza, et al. *Dastanha-ye No*. Tehran: Entesharat-e Shabahang, 1366 [1987].

Ravanipur, Moniru. *Ahl-e Gharq*. Tehran: Khaneh-ye Aftab, 1368 [1989/1990].

Roknzadeh-Adamiyyat, Mohammad Hoseyn. *Daliran-e Tangestani*. 7th ed. Tehran: Entesharat-e Eqbal, 1354 [1975].

Sa'di. *Bustan*. Edited by Nurollah Iranparast, 2d ed. Tehran: Danesh, 1976.

Sa'edi, Gholamhoseyn. Dandil. 3d ed. Tehran: Entesharat-e Amir Kabir, 2535 [1976].

———. *Tars va Larz*. 6th ed. Tehran: Entesharat-e Zaman, 2537 [1978].

Sarabi, Hoseyn ebn-e Abdollah. *Makhzan ol-Vaqaye': Safarnameh-ye Farrokh Khan Aminoddowleh*. Edited by Karim Esfahaniyan and Qodratollah Rowshani. Tehran: Entesharat-e Asatir, 1361 [1982].

Shahani, Khosrow. "Borj-e Tarikhi." *Vahshatabad*. 4th ed. Tehran: Amir Kabir, 2536 [1977].

Shahidi, Homayun, ed. *Safarnameh-ye Shikago: Khaterat-e Haj Mirza Mohammad Ali Mo'inossaltaneh beh Orupa va Amrika*. Tehran: Entesharat-e Elmi, 1363 [1984].

Shirazi (Kazeruni), Mirza Saleh. *Gozaresh-e Safar*. Edited by Homayun Shahidi. Tehran: Mo'asseseh-ye Entesharati-ye Rah-e No, 1362 [1983].

Shushtari, Abdollatif. *Tohfatolalam*. Edited by Samad Movahhed. Tehran: Ketabkhaneh-ye Tahuri, 1363 [1984].

Talebi, Faramarz. *Bargha'i az Fasl-e Khun*. Tehran: Nashr-e Tondar, 1359 [1980].

Talebof, Abdolrahim. *Siyasat-e Talebi*. Edited by Rahim Ra'isniya, Mohammad Ali Aliniya, and Ali Katebi. Tehran: Entesharat-e Elm, 1357 [1978].

Taqva'i, Naser. "Aqa Julu." *Arash* 2, no. 1 (Summer 1964):84–94.

Tavakoli-Targhi, Mohamad. "Asar-e Agahi az Enqelab-e Faranseh dar Sheklgiri-ye Engareh-ye Mashrutiyyat dar Iran." *Iran Nameh* 8 (Summer 1990):411–439.

Zarrinkub, Hamid. *Cheshmandaz-e She'r-e No-ye Farsi*. Tehran: Entesharat-e Tus, 1358 [1979].

INDEX